# Beyond the National Curriculum

WITHDRAWN

Against a background of political, economic and social changes in Europe and the USA, **David Coulby** explores the place of knowledge within society. Coulby looks at the widespread growth of national self-consciousness and the trend towards an increased heterogeneity of society. He argues that this has led to a shift towards curricular centralism and an eagerness for states to specify an homogenous knowledge for their populations.

*Beyond the National Curriculum* focuses on what is taught in schools and universities in Europe and the USA. It considers the role of school and university education in producing prejudice against marginalized groups and citizens of other nations. It also evaluates the role that school and university knowledge plays in the generation of conflict within and between states. This provocative book offers a radical assessment of the role of school and university education, questioning the accepted links between state and knowledge.

**David Coulby** has taught in primary, secondary and special schools. He is currently Professor of Education at Bath Spa University College. He has published on a wide range of educational issues, with a particular focus on intercultural curriculum questions.

**Master Classes in Education Series**
Series Editors: John Head, School of Education,
Kings College, University of London and
Ruth Merttens, School of Education, University of
North London

# Beyond the National Curriculum

Curricular Centralism and Cultural
Diversity in Europe and the USA

David Coulby

London and New York

First published 2000 by RoutledgeFalmer
11 New Fetter Lane, London EC4P 4EE

Simultaneously published in the USA and Canada
by RoutledgeFalmer
29 West 35th Street, New York, NY 10001

*RoutledgeFalmer is an imprint of the Taylor & Francis Group*

Typeset in Garamond by
Curran Publishing Services Ltd
Printed and bound in Great Britain by
TJ International Ltd, Padstow, Cornwall

*British Library Cataloguing in Publication Data*
A catalogue record for this book is available from the British Library

*Library of Congress Cataloging in Publication Data*

Coulby, David.
  Beyond the national curriculum : curricular centralism and cultural diversity in
  Europe and the USA/David Coulby.
  144 pp. 15.6 x 23.4 cm. -- (Master classes in education series)
  Includes bibliographical references and index.
  1. Education--Curricular--Social aspects--Europe. 2. Education--Curricular--
  Social
  aspects--United States. 3. Education and state--Europe. 4. Education and state--
  United States. 5. Multicultural education--Europe. 6. Multicultural
  education--United States.
  I. Title. II. Series.

LB1564.E85 C68 2000
375'.00094--dc21                                        00-020577

ISBN 0-7507-0973-1
     0-7507-0972-3 (pbk)

# Contents

*Contents*

# Series Editors' Preface

It has become a feature of our times that an initial qualification is no longer seen to be adequate for life-long work within a profession and programmes of professional development are needed. Nowhere is the need more clear than with respect to education, where changes in the national schooling and assessment system, combined with changes in the social and economic context, have transformed our professional lives.

The series, Master Classes in Education, is intended to address the needs of professional development, essentially at the level of taught masters degrees. Although aimed primarily at teachers and lecturers, it is envisaged that the books will appeal to a wider readership, including those involved in professional educational management, health promotion and youth work. For some, the texts will serve to update their knowledge. For others, they may facilitate career reorientation by introducing, in an accessible form, new areas of expertise or knowledge.

The books are overtly pedagogical, providing a clear track through the topic by means of which it is possible to gain a sound grasp of the whole field. Each book familiarizes the reader with the vocabulary and the terms of discussion, and provides a concise overview of recent research and current debates in the area. While it is obviously not possible to deal with every aspect in depth, a professional who has read the book should feel confident that they have covered the major areas of content, and discussed the different issues at stake. The books are also intended to convey a sense of the future direction of the subject and its points of growth or change.

In each subject area the reader is introduced to different perspectives and to a variety of readings of the subject under consideration. Some of the readings may conflict, others may be compatible but distant. Different perspectives may well give rise to different lexicons and different bibliographies, and the reader is always alerted to these differences. The variety of frameworks within which each topic can be construed is then a further source of reflective analysis.

The authors in this series have been carefully selected. Each person is an experienced professional, who has worked in that area of education as a practitioner and also addressed the subject as a researcher and theoretician. Drawing upon both pragmatic and theoretical aspects of their experience, they are able to take a reflective view while preserving a sense of what occurs, and what is possible, at the level of practice.

## Beyond the National Curriculum:
## Curriculum Centralism and Cultural Diversity in Europe and the USA

What is it to 'know' something? To what extent is what we know we 'know' bound in with what we believe we are, in terms of our ethnic, national, religious and cultural identity? As teachers and as educators, such questions probe the very heart of what we are about. They allude to the often invisible relationship between what and how we teach and the development of the economy, the state, and both national and global peace. However, within the classrooms in the colleges and schools around the country, such issues are only rarely, if ever, discussed or aired. Most of the time, we remain content to assume that we teach what we know and children learn what we teach, and that questions of politically controlled knowledge within highly diverse populations are not part of the business of education, still less of actual teachers.

An incident reported by a student teacher on teaching practice in a local primary school makes the point. A new entry to the reception class was taking part in a class science lesson. The four-year-old listened as the teacher talked about how some animals no longer existed in the world today. With the aid of pictures, she described the Dodo, what it looked like and where it used to live. 'Has anyone got any idea why the Dodo became extinct?' she asked. The new boy put up his hand. 'Because only one Dodo got into the ark.', he explained. 'No,' replied the teacher gently. 'Has anyone else got any ideas why the Dodo became extinct?' The student teacher commented that what the new child had thought of as 'knowledge' turned out, in the setting of the school, not to count as 'knowledge' at all but as myth. In a more adult but similar example, one still recalls the surprise when, on a college trip to the Bayeux tapestry in Normandy, we realized for the first time that the invasion of England by the wicked Normans could fairly be viewed as a justified insistence that a promise be kept. The English view of the Norman invasion was revealed to us as just that: an 'English view', *part* of our heritage, and simultaneously *partial*.

In this book, Professor Coulby provides us not so much with a series of answers, as a set of complex and pertinent connections. His subject matter, as he explains in his introduction, is the place of knowledge within the changing network of nations and states, of economic dependencies and controls, and of peaceful and warring tendencies. The transitions currently taking place in Europe, markedly different in east and west, are carefully described in order to allow him to develop an analysis of the relations between educational curricula and the bases of traditional, cultural and religious knowledge. He explains how knowledge has emerged as 'a major trading commodity in the international market' and the effects of this upon production and consumption within these 'knowledge-based' economies. At the same time, he traces the growth of postmodernism, which is described as a critical stance, 'a way of regarding the world and oneself'. This increasing and demonstrable distrust of absolute knowledge, of the very possibility of a definitive account or 'voice', echoes the profound economic and political changes taking place post-Thatcher and Regan, in the developed world.

One of us remembers David Coulby lecturing on sociology at the University of North London in the mid 1980s. His students spoke of his contentious statements and of the ways in which he would challenge matters which had previously seemed almost self-evident to them. At the start of this book, he warns the reader that his teaching style is best characterized as 'pedagogy of provocation'. He sets out to help us re-think and re-formulate our ideas about the political control of knowledge, and the ways in which this politically controlled knowledge is in contrast to, or in conflict with, the diversity of the populations to whom it is delivered as institutionalized curricula. In the course of this endeavour, we traverse topics as varied, and as important, as the relation between knowledge and warfare, religious belief, special education needs and identity.

This book provokes and engages, it disturbs and excites. We are not left with the illusions we started with, and neither are we allowed to remain intellectually lazy or politically uninformed. It deals with the very *'raison d'etre'* for education, the distribution and dissemination of knowledge and the enculturation of the children in and of our societies. David Coulby tells us that 'if this text is successful, it will provoke both assent and disagreement'. In the eyes of the editors, it does just that.

*Ruth Merttens and John Head*
November 1999

# Acknowledgements

Although I have been involved in several writing projects, this is the first book that I have written on my own. It seems an appropriate place to acknowledge the various contributions without which it could not have been completed.

Thanks to Ruth Merttens for remembering our conversations and for commissioning this book on behalf of Falmer. Thanks to her too, and to Robert Cowen and Crispin Jones, for commenting on an earlier draft. The sins of omission and commission remain my own.

Many students and lecturers at Bath Spa University College and at the London University Institute of Education have discussed with me the matters central to this book and have helped me develop my understanding. Furthermore, I would wish to add the names of Leslie Bash and Jagdish Gundara to those of Robert Cowen and Crispin Jones as the people who have helped me to understand aspects of society and education.

More than most writers on education I am indebted to academics in foreign parts for doing their best to correct my misunderstandings of their societies, cultures and education systems. Friends and colleagues in the AENEAS network established under SOCRATES and in the various TEMPUS projects in which I have participated have been particularly helpful in this respect. Hospitality and discussions in Madison, Rotterdam, Joensuu, Daugavpils, Oradea, Sibiu, Rethymnon, Athens, Ioannina, Hildesheim, Berlin, Gent, Copenhagen and Sophia are warmly acknowledged.

As well as the people mentioned above, the development of the ideas in this book is particularly due to discussions, often over many years, with Bill Lee, Mike Berger, Nigel Prior, Tony Welsh, Andreas Kazamias, John Raynor, George Flouris, Evie Zambeta and Phil Garner.

I am grateful to Bath Spa University College for establishing a climate in which research and scholarship are encouraged, and to my colleagues in the Faculty of Education and Human Sciences for their support and enthusiasm. In particular I would like to thank Christine Eden, Heather Williamson and Stephen Ward for their unflinching personal, professional and intellectual support across thirteen years.

*Acknowledgements*

Thanks to Jacquie, Emma and Will for supporting this project and for sharing the sometimes esoteric interests on which it is based.

I would like to dedicate this book to the memory of my mother, Emma Coulby, and to my father, Derek, who considered my interest in the link between education and warfare worthy of further investigation.

*David Coulby*

# Introductory Remarks

People tend to assume that what they are taught in schools and universities is true, worthwhile and useful. Having completed their education they will retain the impression that what they learned is what everyone learns and should learn. Few, even among those who work in education, will question the content of schooling and higher education. For example, people will debate and research the most effective ways to teach science, but pay less attention to what science should be taught. They almost totally fail to address the question of whether science should be taught at all. The curricula of schools and universities are taken for granted.

In Europe and the USA the content of the school curriculum is increasingly subject to political, often central, control. There is also a tendency towards greater curricular uniformity, both within countries and between them. Higher education is also part of this trend. Many countries or, in the case of federations like Germany or the USA, states, are developing national curricular systems. In the case of England and Wales this is known as The National Curriculum. This book explores what lies outside the National Curriculum, what has been expelled from it, in cultural and epistemological terms. By focusing on Europe and the USA instead of simply England and Wales it also provides an insight into what lies beyond the National Curriculum in international terms.

The book questions the appropriateness of the shift towards curricular centralism. Furthermore, it questions the appropriateness of the resulting curricula for the societies that they are presumably designed to serve. It does this principally by pointing to the heterogeneous populations of Europe and the USA. The many different cultures of Europe represent different knowledge and value systems that in many cases are radically different from, or even oppositional to, those embodied in national curricula. For people in such groups the content of school and university knowledge is less easily taken for granted since it represents a threat to their culture, even to their very survival as a group.

The book considers the various ways in which curricular systems have deviated from their apparent purpose. It concentrates on those individuals and groups who are victims of state knowledge: those who are disadvantaged by state knowledge and those who are ignored or denigrated by it. It focuses on the distorted identities produced and reproduced, for the privileged as well as the disadvantaged, by deviant knowledge systems.

Curricular systems are also seen to be deviant at a system level. The link between knowledge production and material production is explored against the emergence of a knowledge economy. The state's monopoly of the means of violence and its monopoly over knowledge production and reproduction is explored against the continuity of warfare in Europe. The dissonance between curricula and societies is seen in its most extreme form in those states where schools and universities actually teach hatred of the inhabitants of other states or of non-dominant groups.

Commensurate with its concentration on diversity, the book adopts an international perspective. It attempts to escape the national and nationalist confines of state curricular systems. The exemplification is drawn from across Europe and the United States. By providing an insight into a diversity of knowledge systems it provides some contextualisation of those most familiar to readers. Recognizing that school and university knowledge change when state boundaries are crossed is a further technique in bringing them into closer scrutiny. An international perspective can assist in reversing the process of taking school and university knowledge for granted.

Analysing education from a variety of perspectives, the book develops a cumulative presentation of curricular systems radically at variance with the societies and economies within which they operate. The victims of this variance are many. Among the casualties of centralization is school and university knowledge itself, displaced in too many cases by its opposite, the institutionalization of lies, trivia, ignorance and prejudice.

# 1 Introduction: Transitions in Europe and the Central Role of Knowledge

## Europe in Transition

Some political transitions are highly visible. The destruction of the Berlin wall and its subsequent fate as trophies for western politicians and tourist souvenirs gave visible expression to the collapse of the Iron Curtain, the end of Soviet domination of Eastern Europe and the eventual reunification of Germany. Sometimes the visible moments are themselves misleading. Romania was to wait several years after the demise of Ceaucescu before the *securitate* relaxed its grip on the state and the modernization of the economy and the polity could slowly proceed. Some transitions, by no means less fundamental, are less readily symbolized. Perhaps the big bang which accompanied the liberalization and computerization of the London stock exchange in the mid-1980s might symbolize a new economic order in the United Kingdom and the United States which was quickly followed by the other European Union (EU) states.

Reagan came to power in 1978, Thatcher in 1979. In the period since then the states of the expanding European Union and those of Eastern Europe and the former Soviet Union have all undergone major transitions. With the introduction of the common currency for eleven EU members in 1999 and with the planned expansion of the Union to the east and to the south (accession negotiations are currently proceeding with Estonia, Poland, the Czech Republic, Hungary, Slovenia and Cyprus), along with new accessions to NATO (Hungary, Poland and the Czech Republic joined in 1999), a further period of social and political turbulence is likely. At the same time international capital has never been more footloose. The investment and disinvestment decisions of trans-national corporations are of major importance to the economic prosperity of all European states and to the political stability of many. Meanwhile the latest tranche of information and communications technology (ICT) developments is transforming all modes of production, distribution and consumption. The European countries are in the midst of profound and by no means completed transitions (see many of the chapters in Coulby, Cowen, and Jones (2000).

This chapter attempts briefly to identify and differentiate important features of these transitions. It is against this background that the discussion of knowledge in the succeeding chapters needs to be understood. Unfortunately not everything can be said at once. Inevitably there are terms and concepts used in the opening chapters which are only clarified or problematized later in the text. In particular, 'postmodernism', the notion of a Europe divided between East and West, and the relationships between states and nations are revisited in some depth in later chapters.

Transitions are different between the east and western states. In Eastern Europe features that characterize this transition so far include:

- political freedom
- economic liberalization
- nationalism
- the breakdown of social order
- a renewed interest in the west.

In the United States and Western Europe the features include:

- the reconfiguration of global capitalism
- uncontested US political power
- the rapid development of ICT and the related emergence of the knowledge economy
- 'postmodernism'
- a revised interest in the east.

Of course not all states display all these features. They constitute the generalizations within which individual exemplifications can be identified.

## Eastern Europe in Transition

To take Eastern Europe first, the benefits, or for that matter the extent, of political freedom must not be overstated. Whilst speech, publication, worship and media are certainly substantially freer in a great many states from the Czech republic to Estonia, there are many groups who would question the nature of their new-found freedom: Crimean Tartars, Russian speakers in Latvia, Chechens, Magyar speakers in Serbian Vojvodina to name but a few. Nevertheless, in almost the whole of Eastern Europe there is an exceedingly widespread awareness of a greatly enhanced perspective of personal freedom and renewed political participation. The communist parties themselves have in many cases performed a miraculous transformation into electable democratic groups.

This political liberalization has been the accompaniment, if not the precondition, for economic liberalization. With varying degrees of pain – starvation until recently in winter in Sofia, for example – the Eastern European economies are transforming to participate in the global market. While massive inflows of international capital are still, in most states, eagerly awaited, some economies are on clear convergence with their western neighbours as is recognized by the planned admission of Estonia, Poland, the Czech Republic, Hungary and Slovenia to the EU. A further tranche of east European countries are almost certain to follow. The admission of Poland and Estonia will give the EU further land boundaries with Russia (in addition to the Finland–Karelia border). (NATO is following a similar but not identical pattern of expansion. In both cases there are many more states wishing to join the two international organizations than are currently being accepted.) However, the earlier assumption that the Eastern European economies were on a convergence with those of the west are having to be revised (Pinder 1998). Romania and Bulgaria as well as many of the states of former Yugoslavia have gone into serious economic decline in the 1990s. In economic and indeed political terms the very notion of transition may be seen to be sanguine here (Lieven 1998), unless a substantial time-scale is implied.

In addition to the applications to join NATO and the EU, the renewed interest in the west is also manifested in the expanded membership of the Council of Europe. English and German are already more widely spoken. English language films, television programmes, books, magazines, pop music and software are widely available. Cities such as Cracow or Prague have become the romantic destination of western tourists. With less triumphalism and financial self-assurance the stream of eastern tourists and visitors to the west begins to rise. EU Tempus and Soros Foundation funds have assisted the educational and academic component of this rapprochement and these excursions.

This transition has not been without its downside, the breakdown of social order and the re-emergence of nationalism being among the two most notable aspects. Crime rates have exploded in Sofia as well as in Moscow and St Petersburg. Drug abuse and vandalism have accompanied Microsoft and Coca-Cola into Eastern Europe. Especially for the older generation, there is a widespread perception of a breakdown of social order that, along with the perceived tardiness of western financial and military commitment, provides much of the groundswell towards the born-again communist parties.

The manifestations of re-emergent nationalism have varied from the citizenship laws of the Baltic states and the break-up of Czechoslovakia, to civil wars in Yugoslavia, Georgia and Chechnia (Cohen 1996; Ignatieff 1994; Pavkovic 1997; Lieven 1998). This nationalism has highly particularistic loyalties and is capable of generating the most intense passions. It is exacerbated by apparent economic disparities, between Slovenia and Serbia, or between Czechia and Slovakia. It constitutes a major threat to the stability of many part of the region: currently, Kosovo, Macedonia (FYROM) and Bosnia. Furthermore, Russian nationalism and its uneasy relationship with that of many of its new neighbours, the Baltic states, Georgia, Moldova, and so on, may also come to constitute a continental threat. If the period of transition in Eastern Europe is not to be even bloodier, then some control over nationalist feelings and activities appears to be essential. In addition the economic and political stability of Russia continues to be a matter of concern. Current NATO involvement in Kosovo, combined with economic stagnation, the growth of crime and the resurgence of nationalism in Byelorussia as well as Russia, provides a mixture in which continuing transitions will be, at the least, uneasy.

## Western Europe in Transition

Western European states have undergone rapid economic change. This has involved participation in the global market for labour, finance, goods and services. It has involved a rapid recognition of the economic strength of Japan and of the emergent Asian countries, and responses to this increased competition both by individual states and by the EU. It has recognized the urgent need for inward investment, often from these emergent states. More fundamentally it has seen the evolution towards a knowledge economy, one based on services rather than manufacture. The introduction of ICT into so many processes of financing, design, management, production, distribution and consumption has been a significant stage in this evolution (see, especially, Chapter Five). The countries of the west and of the Pacific rim are attempting, with varying degrees of determination, to transform themselves into 'smart' states.

Knowledge has emerged as a major trading commodity in the international market. Knowledge and knowledge-based processes both underpin material production and are themselves becoming ever more important aspects of production and consumption. Knowledge in fields such as armaments developments, pharmaceutical production and medical techniques is highly sought after across the world. Design of clothing, cars or food can be more remunerative than their manufacture or sale. The media and publications industries now look to global, multi-media production with a string of associated, franchized products. The design of computer systems, and especially software and operating and filing systems, has facilitated the mushrooming of global monopolies. The economies of the EU and the United States are gradually shifting to this knowledge production and reproduction. This gives an increasingly enhanced role to the curriculum of schools and universities. Educational institutions, as is indicated in Chapter Eight, may be in a race between on the one hand meeting the needs of the knowledge economy or on the other hand irrelevance and obsolescence.

The power of the USA has been virtually unchallenged in political terms since the breakup of the Soviet Union. While the economic power of Japan, the latent strength of Russia and the gradual coalescence of Europe all indicate that this is likely to be a temporary phenomenon, it has meant that the fundamental economic transitions are taking place against a background of relative international stability. The systematic global terror of the cold war has been replaced by ongoing neo-colonial adventures such as Desert Storm or Grand Alliance. The latter provides a stark example: NATO (effectively the USA) engaged in the bombardment and invasion of the territory of the former Yugoslavia without apparently risking global conflict. This would have been unimaginable in the cold war context.

'Postmodernism' must at first appear in scare quotes until it is clear that this is not a historical epoch, nor a mode of social solidarity or economic organization but rather a critique, a stance or a way of regarding the world and oneself. Postmodernism is a sceptical, consumerist playfulness, which increasingly describes a wide range of social and cultural phenomenon in the European Union and the United States. It is characterized by:

- a distrust of grand narratives, including progress, science and Marxism
- a tendency to look to give voice to marginalized perspectives, be they those of women, black people, the handicapped (see Chapter Five) or homosexuals
- a tendency to deconstruct dominant discourses and discursive strategies
- a tendency to collage, play and eclectic allusion, particularly in the arts
- a psychology which focuses on identity but only to insist upon its multiplicity
- life styles that self-consciously individualize and commodify taste and culture.

While the political consequences of the profound economic change may have yet to reveal themselves, the eclectic, self-referring, sceptical voice of postmodernism may well be its cultural accompaniment (see especially Chapter Seven).

Just as the events of 1989 and 1991 brought about changed attitudes in the east to the west, so policies and philosophies have adjusted also in the opposite direction. One may hope that the period of western triumphalism is coming to an end. The opportunity is being taken to consolidate the European Union and NATO in the eastern part of the continent, thereby, it is hoped, ensuring continued peace and, if the EU's past record is anything to go by, enhanced prosperity. If this process is carried out smoothly and quickly, it is possible that the not inconsiderable resentment of those likely to be last admitted to the club (Romania, Bulgaria, Bosnia) may be minimized and the danger of their looking again to Moscow may be avoided. In this process of rapprochement the west has had to learn the limits of both its economic wisdom and its political effectiveness, as the record of the Union's interference in Yugoslavian affairs so dismally witnesses. NATO's apparent success in Kosovo is put into perspective by its inability to prevent the destruction of Grozny.

## Education in Times of Transition

Just as states differ in the extent to which they are involved in the transitions described above, so they differ in the extent to which they seek to adapt their education systems to address these changing circumstances. While there certainly are structural aspects to this adaptation – the growth of higher education in the west and the emergence of private institutions in Eastern Europe – it is on curricular aspects that this book concentrates. To what extent have the curricular systems of

Eastern and Western European schools and universities been adapted to recognize and facilitate the wider transitions? In beginning to answer this question, the remainder of this chapter introduces themes that are subsequently developed in the rest of the book.

One of the important curricular responses to transition has been the reformulation of nationalism. This can most readily be seen in terms of languages. Language education was not the only instrument of Russification (Haarmann 1995). Other, less subtle techniques had been used: mass murder and deportation, the influx of Russian speakers, and party or citizenship restrictions on national language speakers. The Soviet approach to asymmetric bilingualism had been at best assimilationist, and at worst attempted the destruction of nations such as the Inguchetians, the Chechens, the Volga Germans and the Crimea Tartars (Khazanov 1995). National language speakers in the three Baltic states felt that their languages too had been taken to the edge of elimination. Language, then, was a critical area of nation building in many of the newly independent states. In Estonia, Latvia and Lithuania, Russian ceased to be the language of many schools and is rapidly being replaced in the universities. The first foreign language ceased to be Russian and became English.

Other important changes involved the abandonment of Marxist-Leninism as the paradigm discourse for a variety of subjects from sociology to biology in schools and universities across the former Soviet Union and Eastern Europe. History too had to be rapidly re-written and Soviet internationalism to be revealed as a further aspect of the centuries long expansion of the Muscovy state. 'In the former Soviet Union,' the joke goes, 'the past is always unpredictable'. Across Eastern Europe paragraphs on Soviet friendship and brotherhood were deleted from history and social science textbooks and replaced by ones on the suppression and ultimate triumph of the national destiny (Silova 1996). (See especially Chapter Four.)

National culture, no longer in the shadow of the Moscow-financed, state-ideologized, culture machine, found itself with a central dimension in the curricula of schools. In Latvia, for instance, folk song and folk dance, manifestations of the rich national tradition, could take up the school time previously given over to dreary, polytechnic wishful thinking. Schools and universities were set free to celebrate the nation, to reinforce the strength of its language, to re-make its history and to re-shape its civil society. In this emancipatory, epistemological transformation, many states are still engaged. Unfortunately there was a down side.

As the example of the Russification of the Soviet Union itself indicates, nation-building and nationalism-building are all too often closely connected. Following 1991, in many states of the former Soviet Union this took the form of the denigration of Russia and all things Russian, which too often had as its political accompaniment harsh restrictions on citizenship (Lieven 1993). In Eastern Europe too the re-writing of history and the celebration of culture too readily focused on a narrow definition of what the nation was, who the true citizens were, and who the historical enemies had been. The rediscovery of the nation and national identity was accompanied by a rediscovery or recreation of the other (UNDP 1995; Cucos 1997; Coulby 1997a). The Serbs reasserted their difference from Bosnians and Croatians; more peacefully the Slovaks revised their distinctiveness. Russians and Chechens threw off the fiction of peaceful, Soviet internationalism. In Latvia, Russian speakers were stripped of their citizenship and many associated human rights. Of course nationalism figures as a continuity as well as a transition. The treatment of Magyars and Gypsies in Romania was little improved in the new democracy from their conditions under the xenophobic Ceaucescu regime.

In this reassertion of nationalism the schools and universities played their parts. A surprising number of the most fervent Serbian nationalists, the architects of ethnic cleansing and the proponents of Greater Serbia were university academics (Judah 1997). In the invention of tradition, the school and university curricula stressed a particular view of history, the Battle of Kosovo, say, or the 1939–45 period, which identified peoples of other languages, scripts or religions as others; in extreme cases as enemies. The sense of solidarity invoked by literary masterpiece, folk song or common enjoyment of sacred landscape has too readily become a sense of solidarity against the other (see, especially, Chapter Seven). The shift to English as the second language is leading to the neglect of the other languages of the state and of near neighbours. The unfortunate and, in some instances disastrous, concomitants of reawakened national identity have been revived xenophobia and regional isolationism: a process in which school and university curricula have played a significant part.

Faced with the political, economic and cultural uncertainties of a period of transition, many states in the west as well as the east have attempted to consolidate traditional values within the school curriculum. The National Curriculum in England and Wales is an obvious example (see, especially Chapter Two). Others would include the Hellenocentric stress in the Greek curriculum (Allison and Nicolaidis 1997; Chouliaras 1993; Flouris 1995; Flouris 1996; Flouris 1997; Flouris 1998; Massialas 1995; Massialas and Flouris 1994) or the persistence of confessional religious teaching in the schools of many states of the EU and its reappearance in Eastern Europe.

It would appear that, partly as a result of misunderstanding the nature of the transitions, and partly out of resistance to them, states have consolidated traditionalist and modernist elements within their school curricula (see, especially Chapter Three). In many instances, such as Serbia, England and Wales, or Greece, this has been conflated with that ongoing or revived nationalism identified above, to provide a curriculum both unsuited to the needs of the knowledge economy and potentially or actually destructive of democratic pluralism.

The subject of this book then is the connections and disconnections between knowledge, society, the economy and power: between books, people, money and guns. In particular it examines:

- the political control of knowledge
- the relationship of politically controlled knowledge to the developing economy
- the tension between centralist political knowledge and highly diverse populations.

## Exemplification and Rhetorical Devices

The patient reader will have already noticed a certain idiosyncrasy in the choice of examples. This chapter has so far made several references to Latvia and none to much larger and more obviously important states such as Germany, France, Italy or Spain. This is not a choice of those states whose politics, culture and educational systems are better known to me personally. Rather it is that some states in Europe best exemplify particular curricular characteristics: Latvia, dramatic curricular change; Greece, the state control of knowledge; Serbia and England and Wales, ethnocentricity. Inevitably, given the authorship and much of the readership of the volume, there is discussion in the succeeding chapters of the National Curriculum in England and Wales. But there is also a range of reference to many other European countries and to the United States. This is by no means an attempt at comparative education in the old style (for example, King 1979), an illumination of policy issues at home by investigating their treatment elsewhere. Rather the book is an analysis of an issue (the relationship between money, guns and books) with illustrations from a wide variety of contexts, allowing for both generalization and particularism. Thus there are no conventional comparativist taxonomies, rather an internationally illustrated exploration of a major educational theme. I have tried to take a view of the whole of Europe and have drawn exemplification, where possible and relevant, from the states of Eastern Europe and the former Soviet Union.

The topic is complex and no statement in this area is likely to be final or exhaustive. This book attempts to address the main issues from a variety of perspectives. While the opening chapters (Two, Three and Four) discuss directly the formation of state knowledge, others address it more obliquely: through the emergence of the knowledge society (Five); through the perspective of people perceived to have special needs (Six) or through its impact on peace and war (Seven) or on identity formation (Eight). Thus the book slices its apple from a variety of different angles.

Much of the content of this book is developed from courses I have taught at the London Institute of Education and at Bath Spa University College, as well as papers presented to international conferences and seminars. My students at Bath have (correctly) identified my teaching style as the pedagogy of provocation. I try to say things in such a way that students are encouraged to re-think their often long- and firmly-held ideas; to make them challenge what I am saying as a way of better understanding both my views and their own. There was a temptation in writing this book to tone down the rhetoric and to some extent I have succumbed. I left intact, however, the description of the curricula of Europe and the United States as 'lies and nonsense' in the final chapter and, as the patient reader has perhaps already noticed, I have retained some of my tendency to sharpness of illustration and to overstatement. This is deliberate. If this text is successful it will provoke both assent and disagreement, each doubtless earnestly held and vigorously argued.

## Discussion Questions

1   Is it possible to distinguish the features that have led some former eastern block countries into relative prosperity and others into civil war and lawlessness?
2   To what extent are school and university curricula legitimate policy implements for the task of nation building?
3   To what extent is the discourse of transitions appropriate to Eastern Europe and the former Soviet Union, or to the EU and the USA?
4   Does the chapter imply that major political and economic changes necessitate changes in education systems? Is this assumption correct?

## Further Reading

As I was completing this book I was also editing a volume in the *World Yearbook of Education* series on the theme of transitions: Coulby, D., Cowen, R. and Jones, C. (eds) (2000) *The World Yearbook of Education 2000: Education in Times of Transition*, London: Kogan Page. This deals with the different nature of transitions in different states and the ways they have impacted on education policy.

I was lucky in that one of the first books I read on the transition in Eastern Europe and the former Soviet Union was Lieven's compelling account of the Baltic States: Lieven, A. (1993) *The Baltic Revolution: Estonia, Latvia, Lithuania and the Path to Independence*, New Haven: Yale University Press. The relative smallness and remoteness of Estonia, Latvia and Lithuania should in no way be seen to lessen their importance. Lieven's volume is actually about the break-up of the whole Soviet Union. For students of education he charts some striking examples of the invention of tradition. His later book on Chechnya is again highly illuminating for the insight that it throws on the situation in Russia itself: Lieven, A. (1998) *Chechnya: Tombstone of Russian Power*, New Haven and London: Yale University Press.

For an overview of the former Soviet Union, see also: Khazanov, A. K. (1995) *After the USSR: Ethnicity, Nationalism and Politics in the Commonwealth of Independent States*, Madison: University of Wisconsin Press.

# 2  The State Control of Knowledge

## Knowledge Selection and Knowledge Selectors

It is the argument of this book that there is a tension between what is taught in the schools and universities of the states of Europe and the nature of the populations of those states. This tension places, on one side of the argument, curricular systems, now increasingly centralized and state-controlled, and, on the other, human diversity in its many forms. This diversity is becoming progressively more self-conscious in terms of nationality, racial identity and so on. The tension itself has varying degrees of intensity. At some levels, in some states, there is an attempt to diminish it by reflecting and enhancing the social diversity of the region or the continent within curricular systems. In other states, by contrast, the tension may be manifested in such extreme forms as the maintenance, by state controlled curricular systems, of prejudice against people perceived to have special educational needs, or the encouragement by schools and universities of racism and xenophobia.

All curricular systems are a selection from the vastness of human knowledge. What humanity knows and what it thinks it knows has been amassed, revised and refined across many centuries. Those in charge of curriculum definition must make a tiny selection from this voluminous and diverse material. For pupils who only undergo the compulsory years of schooling this selection is particularly small. Beyond that, in the later years of schooling and at university, students themselves have some say in the selection process. At the same time the nature of the selection becomes increasingly specialized. The Library of Congress is a vast repository of human knowledge. It receives, for instance, a copy of almost every book and learned journal published in English in the United States and many other countries. Shelf upon shelf, stack upon stack, room upon room, floor upon floor filled with volumes of what humanity considers to be knowledge. Replete with truth and error. The task of those in charge of defining the school and/or university curriculum may be compared to someone going into the Library of Congress and selecting thirty volumes, say, which are to constitute official knowledge for whole generations of children and young people within a particular state. For those who go on to advanced and university level study a few more specialized volumes will be chosen;

the students may even have a say in which they will be, or perhaps be offered some alternatives. For all pupils and young people, what is not selected will be vastly greater than what is. The process of selection, then, is a serious and responsible task: perhaps arrogant, perhaps comical. Those making this selection will have to operate particular criteria, perhaps overt, perhaps concealed or even unrecognized. These criteria may be referred to as knowledge protocols.

Across Europe and the United States there is a predictable sameness about many areas of human knowledge which are excluded from this selection process, and do not confirm to widely applied knowledge protocols. The history, political organization, culture, science and medicine of China, for instance, will be largely neglected. The huge bibliography of Marxist writing, once so assiduously developed in Western as well as Eastern Europe, will be allowed to gather dust (see Chapter Eight). The number system of the Maya civilization will be touched on only briefly. On the other hand, there will also be some sameness as to what is included in curricular systems. The number system currently used in Europe and largely derived from the Arabs will be ubiquitous. The English language will be almost as pervasive. It is unlikely that the process of photosynthesis will be neglected and there will be widespread attention to the achievements of a group of people who lived in Athens in the fourth century BCE. Of course the differences between the selections made in the different states of Europe are themselves as interesting and revealing as the wider level of homogeneity, but the first impression is of a good deal of conformity between states.

Given the importance of this process of adopting knowledge protocols and subsequently selecting curricular, it is important to know which interests are represented in the formation of school and university knowledge. Certainly there are many constituencies in the different states that might consider themselves to have a legitimate voice in this process:

- academics, researchers and those who consider themselves to be at the cutting edge of knowledge in each particular subject
- philosophers or sociologists of knowledge who believe themselves to have an overview of the whole domain of human knowledge
- teachers and those who count themselves competent in the ways in which children learn, who tend to adhere to the notion that the nature of the process of learning must in some ways help to shape the material which is learned
- employers in industry, business and the public sector who must ultimately receive the pupils and students, and who might believe that the tasks of the workplace necessitate the prior acquisition of particular skills and knowledge
- parents and children and young people themselves who would be likely to have a view on what knowledge was relevant to their particular family or group, importantly but not exclusively in such matters as religion, culture and history
- educational managers and inspectors who might also consider themselves as

having a view both of the nature of knowledge as a whole and of the capacity of their particular system to incorporate it
- pressure groups concerned with the environment, with the eradication of world poverty or the treatment of old people and so on might wish for their issue or stance to be covered within the curriculum
- religious authorities might have strong views not only on what belief systems should and should not be taught but also on much wider issues such as the theory of evolution
- politicians from a wide variety of standpoints who regard school and university knowledge as being fundamental not only to the reproduction of economic processes and democratic freedom but also to the formation of individual and social identity, not least national identity.

This list is by no means exhaustive nor are these groups necessarily distinct. Academics and politicians, as well as parents, may be highly influenced by the views of, say, religious authorities. Coming from any of these groups, people might have varying and indeed conflicting views on what should be taught in schools. An interesting example is provided by the enquiry that was set up to investigate the racially motivated murder of a boy, Ahmed Iqbal Ullah, in the playground of Burnage High School in Manchester. The report describes an incident where a primary teacher in a multicultural school had been teaching a class about the celebration of Eid. As part of this lesson all the children had painted a mark on the backs of their hand. At the end of the day an indignant white parent came to see the teacher complaining about the henna mark and its reference to a particular religion. This is the mother's account:

> I became extremely upset and annoyed one day . . . when my son came out of his classroom with a symbol like a star shaped on his hand. I said to him 'what's this' and he said 'we've had a Pakistani party'. I said 'what do you mean' and he replied 'I don't know, but I had to have this on my hand'. I went into the classroom and I said to Miss B 'who has put this on his hand' and she replied 'It's just to celebrate Eid'. I said 'I don't want this on his hand or anything like it ever again'. My words were, I think 'don't ever disfigure my son again'.
>
> (Macdonald et al. 1989: 323–4)

This, then, is one parent's clear line on curriculum content. It would not be difficult to discover similar incidents and trenchantly expressed views in Marseilles or Copenhagen. Interestingly it was the view of those who wrote the report that ultimately the child has a right to knowledge whatever the prejudices of the parents: 'The role of the school is, in our view, to teach the children and not just to bend to parents' prejudices, even if these are elevated into the lofty theory of parental choice' (Macdonald et al. 1989: 401).

Similar reservations may be outlined for the other constituencies that consider themselves to have important roles in the formulation of school and university knowledge. Specialist academics are all too likely to be partial to their own subject and to wish it to have a preponderant part in the school and university curriculum. Their very specialism might itself preclude them from the broad overview needed in the definition of the shape and structure of curricular systems. They may be concerned with large amounts of specialist subject content that readily leads to overcrowded and cluttered curricula. The comical introduction of the first National Curriculum in England and Wales provides an example here. In 1989 groups of supposed experts were convened for each of the politically favoured subjects to draw up the curriculum content for children from five to sixteen. Inevitably they insisted that children and young people should learn lots and lots of their particular subject. This then became law and teachers and pupils spent the next five years struggling bravely with an impossibly overcrowded timetable (Bash and Coulby 1989; Coulby and Bash 1991; Lawton 1988).

Similarly, employers might be unduly concerned with the skills and knowledge needed in their particular line of work. Or, taken as a whole, employers' groups might still be over-concerned with the instrumentalist aspects of the curriculum, preferring to stress basic workplace skills and ignoring both more advanced knowledge and the need for the development of social and individual identity. They might further wish to provide young people with the skills and understanding appropriate for the workplace of yesterday and today but not for that of tomorrow. The views of any particular pressure group, then, can all too readily become narrowly partisan, ignoring wider social, economic and global contexts.

The point is that the appropriate contents of the school and university curriculum are disputed within and between these interest groups. These conflicts will be more strident in some states and in some curricular areas and levels than in others.

## Level of Control, Rigour of Control

In many countries, such as Greece, Norway or France, it is taken almost for granted that the curricula of schools, at least, should be controlled by the state. Greece provides an example of just how extensive this control can be. Greek schools operate their curriculum through a series of textbooks. These textbooks are drawn up by the Pedagogical Institute on behalf of the government. The Institute will consult academics and teachers when it draws up particular textbooks, but the ultimate say on content rests with the Ministry of National Education and Religions. The teachers in schools must teach each subject almost exclusively from the textbooks. For every child at each level throughout Greece, from the islands of the Aegean to the mountains of upper Epirus, there will be certain sections of a range of (the same) textbooks to be covered every term. The teachers and the parents, then, have virtually no say whatsoever in the content of the school curriculum, which is almost exclusively top-down. Any person or group wishing to influence the curriculum would be wasting their time lobbying individual teachers or headteachers, and would need to operate rather at the level of the Ministry of National Education and Religions in Athens.

Greece is only an extreme example here; it is by no means in isolation. In France all schoolbooks, though not centrally produced, must be approved by the central ministry in Paris. Similarly in Spain, where school education has now been devolved to the seventeen autonomous communities, central control and even production of textbooks is still currently maintained. Hungary may be described as a bipolar system where the two levels of power are the central state and the actual school itself (Szabio 1993). One of the levels of control which the state has retained in an otherwise largely devolved system is the curriculum, and in particular the approval of school texts. Spain and Hungary immediately raise the issue of the level of control of educational systems. In Germany, for instance, although there is a good deal of voluntary collaboration, education is effectively devolved to the sixteen *lander*. Within these sixteen systems, however, the level of curricular control is high, with all textbooks having to be approved at *lander* level. Similarly in Switzerland (Szaday 1994), where there is no central ministry of education, curriculum control is at the level of the twenty-six different canton systems. Yet even within these often quite small systems, there is in many cases extreme control, with compulsory textbooks, and teachers often forbidden to select their own texts. According to the organization of the particular state, then, the curriculum can be controlled at central, provincial or local level. Devolution of the curriculum does not imply any relaxation of control. This can be just as rigorous in highly devolved systems such as Switzerland as in highly centralized ones such as Greece or France.

An opposite example of a loosely controlled curriculum system would be hard to find in Europe today but it may, by way of illustration, be located in the primary schools of England and Wales prior to the implementation of the 1988 Education Reform Act. Here the schools, and in many case the individual teachers, had almost total freedom over what they wished to teach. There would be guidelines from Local Education Authorities (LEAs) and some loose and infrequent inspection by central government but there were no statutory guidelines as to which subjects should be covered, what material should be dealt with in each subject, what was appropriate to a particular level, how one year's work led into another's, how learning should be planned and assessed, what feedback on progress should be made to parents and pupils. A teacher with a particular interest in dogs could devise a canine curriculum for a class for an entire term and expect the only response to be the raised eyebrows of colleagues or the headteacher. The idea of a specified textbook would have been anathema in this secret garden. Unlike the Greek system that of England and Wales before 1989 was characterized by a high level of trust in teachers. It was assumed that, as a result of their own education and training, their professional ethos and the rigorous environment of each school, they would know what was the appropriate material to teach to children at each stage of primary education. Anyone wishing to change the curriculum in a system such as this could safely ignore the central authority in London and seek rather to lobby individual teachers or headteachers.

The point here is not only to make an old-style comparative education contrast between centralized and decentralized curricular systems, but rather to show that curricular control can be operated at various levels. The emphasis is on the direction which educational policy is taking across Europe, where, whatever the level of control, its rigour appears to be tightening. While the current reforms of the Greek education system seek to modernize the school curriculum, they do not attempt to give more authority to the teachers. The textbook curriculum will continue, albeit with updated texts. By contrast to earlier practice, in England and Wales a centralized National Curriculum has been rigorously enforced, specifying in minute detail what is to be covered in primary and secondary schools. Furthermore, the control of the curriculum of teacher education courses in the UK and the monitoring of curricula and standards across all university departments, as is the case in Romania, might well indicate that the tertiary curriculum is also moving towards central state control. Finally, with the introduction of the National Literacy Strategy and the National Numeracy Strategy in England and Wales in 1998 and 1999 respectively, not only the curriculum but the actual pedagogy of many lessons is being spelled out in detail for a deskilled, demoralized and over-scrutinized teaching force. Centralized systems are remaining centralized and tightly controlled. Decentralized systems are either centralizing quickly or at least retaining and enhancing their broad control.

For schools this centralization and rigid control has taken the form of the detailed specification of the curriculum, often with learning targets set for children and young people and frequent monitoring of performance, conducted in England and Wales on a national basis. For tertiary education, as yet, central control has been in the main rather less specific. There has, however, been some concern about perceived standards, especially in bipartite systems like the Netherlands, Belgium and Germany, as well as in states such as Romania, where private universities have appeared since the demise of the control economy. This has led to the appearance of quality control mechanisms. Cowen's collection illustrates the strengthening role of these agencies in a range of different states (Cowen 1996a). Many current developments are leading to a greater transparency and potentially greater homogeneity in university programmes:

- the emergence of modular programmes
- the reciprocal recognition of qualifications between European Union (EU) states
- the entrenchment of the EU's European Credit and Transfer Scheme (ECTS)

- the development in non-UK, non-Irish universities of English language programmes and modules to meet the requirements of ERASMUS/ SOCRATES students and those from beyond Europe.

While states may remain cautious about what actually constitutes university knowledge, they are increasingly less shy about stipulating how long it should take to acquire. Romania and the Netherlands are two of the many states determined, for obvious financial reasons, to drive down the amount of time it requires to obtain a first degree.

## Advantages of State-Controlled Curricular Systems

Of course, in one way, there is nothing sinister about the state taking or maintaining firm control of curricular systems. As discussed earlier, the content of school and university curricula is the subject of much conflict and controversy. In democracies, when controversies become entrenched and important they are arbitrated through the ballot box. It may be that duly elected national or regional governments are the only constituencies with the authority and mandate to take charge of school and university knowledge. Certainly there are advantages to state-controlled curricular systems:

- demands made on teachers are clear and explicit, and teachers may well require less advanced or less wide education themselves
- the system is transparent to parents and to pupils; they know what they will be studying and how and when they will be assessed; work at home can assist in this process
- there is continuity between school years and between phases; pupils are unlikely to engage in futile repetition, or alternatively to miss out areas considered important by curriculum planners
- there is continuity between schools in different cities or areas; pupils' curricula do not change when they have to change school; this advantage increases, the further the control is moved towards the central state
- the curriculum is appreciably less open to idiosyncrasy or whimsy; the canine curriculum is apparently excluded
- state level assessment arrangements allow individual schools to be compared against apparently objective criteria; this may be used as a way of claiming value for educational money, or accusing poorly performing schools of unjustified extravagance
- similarly the system as a whole can be monitored year on year to detect apparent improvement or deterioration
- conflict about the curriculum can be resolved by the democratic mechanism of the electoral system.

## Disadvantages of State-Controlled Curricular Systems

There are, however, possibly less obvious, disadvantages to state-controlled knowledge. Three of these must be examined: the de-professionalization of teachers; the dissonance between state and local priorities; the politicization and potential atrophy of knowledge.

There is in the USA as well as Europe an established concern about the de-skilling and de-professionalization of teachers. Three examples from Greece, England and Wales and the five new *Lander* of Germany illustrate the forms that this process can take.

In Greece teaching is regarded as a relatively well-paid and secure job. Teachers can wait for as long as ten years after qualification to obtain teaching posts (Kontogiannopoulou-Polydories and Zambeta 1997). There is thus a lag between the freshness and vigour of their own education and training and the commencement of their work in state schools. Partly as a result of this, the teaching force is basically conservative in both political and educational matters. Teachers are largely happy to be the aparatchiks of the textbook curriculum, not considering themselves to have any legitimate role in consideration of the way in which Greek school knowledge is constructed (Flouris 1998).

While this is an ongoing situation of de-professionalization, that in England and Wales is the result of a radical change of policy on the part of central government. The processes whereby the politicians and civil servants of Westminster and Whitehall invaded the secret garden of the curriculum have been developing since at least 1983, and are not yet completed (Coulby and Ward 1996). It is doubtful if even those making the early policy changes could have foreseen just how far the process would go. Indeed, those responsible for implementing the first round of the National Curriculum frequently emphasized, in order to placate professional fears, the fact that teachers remained in control of pedagogy, of the way in which subjects should be taught in schools. In 1983 the Conservative government sent out draft guidelines for the content of the university and college courses which were responsible for training and educating future teachers. These led to the first centralization of university courses in the United Kingdom (Circular 3/84). This apparently small political change had immense implications: first, it established the precedent of central curricular control from Whitehall; second, it carried the widely publicized implication that the teaching profession was in a mess and that teachers were not properly equipped for their task. This second implication was important, contributing – along with unpopular and unsuccessful industrial action by teachers – to the subsequent erosion of their curricular control. The implementation of the National Curriculum in 1989 was followed by ever closer monitoring of schools through OFSTED inspections, by the publication of test results and compilation of national league tables and ultimately by the National Literacy and Numeracy Strategies. The message (it is no longer appropriate to speak in terms of implications) is clear: teachers in England and Wales cannot be trusted to determine what should be taught in schools nor how it should be taught.

Following the reunification of Germany the position of academics in the five new *Lander* came under close scrutiny. Marxist-Leninism was a totally discredited discourse (Jaraunsch et al. 1997). Yet it had provided the orientation for many East German academics, and of course for those in other states, east and west, in fields as diverse as economics, philosophy and art history. Across the universities of the former East Germany whole departments were closed down, Marxist intellectuals were expelled from their university positions, often to be replaced by ideologically pure colleagues from the west. The fact that political change led to a radical change in university knowledge exemplifies one of the major themes of this book. In terms of de-professionalization, however, there was another message here for German teachers and academics. The process served to remind them that they are civil servants and that, at whatever level, they are firmly within the control of the central state. Even in the case of the German university, academic autonomy has its limits.

The dissonance between local and national priorities might be seen as an unfortunate consequence of centralized curricular policy. As recognized earlier, once issues in a democracy have become contested, the means of arbitration is frequently and appropriately the ballot box. The question is rather which ballot box. In highly centralized systems it is only through votes at a national or general election that curricular policy can be changed. Yet this is rarely a crucial plank of political parties at general elections. Although a party's curricular policy may sometimes be made explicit, national elections are usually won and lost on such matters as economic or defence policy, seen as being of overarching importance to both individual families and the state as a whole. By virtue of voting to join NATO or to decrease income tax, the electorate finds itself inadvertently saddled with a particular version of school and university knowledge. It may be that regional or local elections would be a more appropriate place to determine curricular content, though, as noted earlier this can result in equally rigorous levels of control. In such elections major economic and strategic issues are not up for decision: educational policy then takes on a more enhanced importance and is more likely to be the subject of explicit debate and scrutiny. The appropriate level of decision making within democracies is a delicate topic, and becoming increasingly contested as more decisions are transferred to the emergent authority of the EU. The centralist tendency in Greece or England and Wales, however, may be contrasted with more federal policies in Germany, Spain and Switzerland.

As subsequent chapters will discuss, there is more at stake here than the appropriate level of decision making. In European states many groups with strong identities in terms of language, tradition and culture are regionally based: Magyars in Transylvania, Albanian speakers in North-East Greece, Dutch speakers in the Flemish part of Belgium. Where curricular decisions are made centrally groups such as these may consider that their vital interests – the continuation of their language, religion or culture – are at stake. The centralization of curricular decision making to the level of state general election may be seen to endanger their group identities and civil liberties. Of course this will depend on the political nature of the central state. In Brussels the linguistic rights of the Dutch speakers, and of the German speakers in the east, are maintained and extended in the school and university curriculum. Similarly in Spain the regional governments have control of educational decisions and it is now possible, as was by no means the case under Franco, to be taught to university level in Catalan in Barcelona. Serbian speakers in Croatia or Magyars in Cluj are not so fortunate.

The final potential disadvantage of centralized curricular systems is the politicization and even atrophy of school and university knowledge. It is often easier to identify the politicization of knowledge in other systems than one's own. The flow and ebb of Marxist-Leninism or the Islamicization of school knowledge are ready targets for those who perceive politicization to involve any kind of knowledge system other than the one to which they themselves adhere. Certainly systems in rapid transition such as those in Eastern Europe or the former Soviet Union are ideal examples in which to identify political processes at work on the curriculum. (See Chapter Three for severe reservations about the political discourse of 'eastern' and 'western' Europe.) The Soviet curriculum in Latvia in the period 1945 to 1991, with its partiality for Russification (Haarmann 1995) as well as for Marxist-Leninism, could hardly be characterized as unpoliticized. The curricular transition that followed independence after 1991, however, allows other political processes to be made visible in the process of school reform: Marxist knowledge was unceremonially junked; Latvian became the favoured language of instruction at all levels; English replaced Russian as the favoured foreign language. Equally significantly folk music and dance – which had been crucial repositories and manifestations of national identity during the years of Russification – became important and highly esteemed elements in the school curriculum (Coulby 1997b; Dreifelds 1996; Lieven 1993; Stamers 1993). The politicization of the curriculum means that certain political conflicts, such as asymmetric bilingualism, can be transferred to educational institutions. The subject of history will almost inevitably be contrived to suit political exigencies. This is not merely a matter of party politics, though it can be that: all governments in the United Kingdom and Portugal will have difficulty with curricular presentation of the slave trade and imperialism, as will those in Germany with the 1933–45 period, or with 1922–44 in Italy.

Centralized curricula are vulnerable to shifts in political power. When Kenneth Clark became Secretary of State for Education and Science, one of his duties was the finalization of the National Curriculum for history. Considering himself something of an expert in the area, he announced that history ended in the 1960s and that everything after that was current affairs and should not be taught in schools. This was done against the advice of the relevant working group and amounted to little more than the curricular imposition of personal prejudice. And this was not a result of a change of government but followed a mere cabinet reshuffle. When New Labour came to power in 1997 they did not make an immediate grab for the National Curriculum. They waited for the appropriate period of review. When the Labour revisions appeared they were broadly in line with the traditionalistic framework (Department for Education and Employment 1999). They did, however, make compulsory the teaching of citizenship, an initiative unthinkable under, say, the Thatcher regime. In centralized curricular systems knowledge can change as governments change.

The issue of the politicization of school and university knowledge, then, is no less present in those educational systems in which the processes of transition are less visible and rapid. Liberal democracy, citizenship, capitalist economic progress: these are political values which are espoused by curricular systems, not least in universities, with varying degrees of explicitness, in many states of Europe east now as well as west. Indeed many of the EU's Tempus initiatives have been directly concerned with the transfer of just these values from educational institutions in the west to those in the east. The links between capitalist democratic values in schools and universities and the formation of identity within a consumerist society, or with the legitimization of NATO defence policy, are ones which it will fall to other chapters in this volume to address. At this stage it is sufficient to acknowledge that liberalism, democracy, capitalism, individualism are themselves ideas and ideals which are politically and historically situated. They do not constitute curricular absolutes. They are not necessarily inextricably linked, in the schools and universities of Europe, with the betterment and perfection of the human race.

Finally, politicization entails the risk that school and university knowledge may become stale and unresponsive to research developments, and can ultimately atrophy. Lysenko biology (exclusively stressing environment and minimizing the importance of genetics), as taught for a long time in schools and universities of the Soviet Union, provides an easy example of the way in which the knowledge which higher education developed, worked well to support and enhance a particular political ideology even if it subsequently proved to be of no scientific standing. The ways in which governments and large corporations can control, amplify or silence research agenda are obvious: in the UK research into missile technology or explosives has been encouraged; that into the causes and spread of BSE has received notably less sponsorship. In schools centralized curricula can become stale, remote from the experiences and culture of either the pupils or the teachers. Whilst Franco's Spain, the Greece of the colonels or Salazar's Portugal provide the readiest western examples of this atrophy, it is a danger in all systems where the people who define the knowledge protocols and select school and university curricula are remote from those who are subjected to them. This is rather different from those many states where education is used as an institution of linguistic or cultural imperialism (certainly the case in fascist Spain). It is more a matter of state knowledge becoming arid and remote from all pupils, not merely those of a particular group.

## England and Wales

Given these not inconsiderable disadvantages presented by highly centralized curricular systems, it is perhaps worth pausing to consider how and why England and Wales have, in the last ten years, opted to go so far and so fast in this direction. The changes were, and still are, legitimized by politicians within the discourse of standards. The media in England, television as well as newspapers, have long been hostile to schools and to a rather nebulously perceived 'educational establishment'. There is a persistence and virulence to this hostility that is different from the way education is depicted in other European states or from that in Scotland or Wales. The media, of course, are not responsible for the changes but they created a climate for the political reading of selective statistics concerning standards (Jones 1989). This reading involves comparators across time in the UK itself, and international comparators with standards in other industrialised countries. The reform process was initiated by the Conservative government in the mid-1980s (Chitty 1992; Chitty and Simon 1993). Given that most of the Conservative politicians had themselves been educated at fee-paying schools and insisted on the same for their children, it is not surprising that many of them shared, and indeed fed, the distaste of the English media for state schools and state teachers. Political and journalistic opinion had evinced a distrust and dislike for state schools and teachers which fissiparous trade unions and unsuccessful strike action had done little to modify. Thus the de-professionalization of teachers described above was not an unintended consequence of the reform process but rather one of its more important targets.

There was, in addition, a straight political motivation for the changes. The old system had been characterized as a national system locally administered, and this administration was in the hands of LEAs. These elected bodies, especially in the large cities, were predominantly controlled by Labour. They were avidly and enthusiastically pursuing policies contrary to, or at least divergent from, those of the central Conservative government. In this they were skilfully led by the Inner London Education Authority (ILEA) with its effective built-in Labour majority. In the early to mid-1980s these LEAs were implementing policies for multicultural, anti-racist, anti-sexist and occasionally integrationist curricula. Through initiatives concerning the opening of access, part-time degree study and modularization, they were also influencing curricula in the polytechnics (now universities) which were then in their control. These initiatives were apparently supported by the urban electorate which, partly as a result of central government unpopularity, continued to support Labour at the local level. The 1988 Education Reform Act attacked the very centre of Labour control over education and the curriculum. The National Curriculum took knowledge away from LEAs, schools and teachers, and spelt the demise of progressive, anti-prejudicial curriculum initiatives. The ILEA was abolished and broken up. The polytechnics were removed from LEA control and became independent. By centralizing the curriculum through the 1988 Act, the Conservatives removed control from their political enemies and gave it to themselves in central government and their friends and supporters in the innumerable quangos that were subsequently formed to draw up and regulate the National Curriculum. Labour's impact on education had been dramatically turned back but at the expense of curricular rigidity as well as loss of local control and decision making. Once Labour itself gained control of central government its politicians were as unlikely as their Conservative predecessors to relinquish such a large and important area of power. The way these powers are to be handled is still to be determined but government control of primary pedagogy, mentioned earlier, and another, even more specific, tranche of regulations for teacher education (Department for Education and Employment 1998) do not appear to imply any tendency towards decentralization.

Scotland and Northern Ireland, along with fee-paying schools, are not subject to the National Curriculum. It is England and Wales that provide this *locus classicus* for the process of curricular centralization. The next chapter examines the nature of the populations of the states of Europe and the ways in which their diversity runs counter to curricular homogenization.

## Discussion Questions

1   In democratic societies, who should be responsible for the determination of the school and university curriculum?
2   Are there any overarching principles on which this determination could objectively be made?
3   Is this chapter impartial on the advantages and disadvantages of centralized curricular systems?
4   Is the chapter correct in identifying England and Wales as *locus classicus* of the centralized curriculum? Is the chapter justified in describing the introduction of this National Curriculum as comical?

## Further Reading

Like many students of my generation I was profoundly influenced by Michael Young's collection of essays which drew the attention of sociologists of education away from the structures of schooling and onto the contents of the curriculum: Young, M. F. D. (ed.) (1971) *Knowledge and Control: New Directions for the Sociology of Education*. London: Collier Macmillan. This text remains a classic in that it illustrates the contested relationships between the processes of knowledge formation and of social control.

This chapter grew out of my earlier work attempting to chronicle and analyse the development of the National Curriculum in England and Wales. It will be apparent to the reader that my enthusiasm for this initiative has not been high. The writing that I have published on this theme, often in collaboration, is largely listed in the bibliography.

# 3 Cultural Diversity and State Knowledge

## A Distinction: National Diversity and Urban Diversity

The diversity of the European population may be described as having two different forms: national diversity and urban diversity. The description and exemplification of these forms of diversity in Europe is the main theme of this chapter.

National diversity is exceedingly ancient. The opening chapter eschewed the use of the term 'nation state'. No state in Europe is a nation and no nation is a state. States disguise themselves as nations as a mode of legitimation. Nations take control of states often to the detriment of other nations within their boundaries.

> The relationship between states and nations is everywhere an embattled one. It is possible to say that in many societies, the nation and the state have become one another's projects. That is while nations (or more properly groups with ideas about nationhood) seek to capture or co-opt states and state power, states simultaneously seek to capture and monopolise ideas about nationhood.
>
> (Appadurai 1990: 303)

No state in Europe is contiguous with a nation. Many nations in Europe are scattered across more than one state. The exemplifications provided below are intended to break down any sense of Europe, first the west and then the east, as being composed of unified and homogenous nations politically organized as states.

Urban diversity, at least at its contemporary levels, is a relatively recent phenomenon. It results from people from the south and east of Europe, and from the rest of the world, moving to the cities of the north-west in order to find better political and particularly economic conditions. It may also be used to characterize the movement of Russian people in the Soviet period into the cities of the Baltic States, the Ukraine and Georgia. Here economic factors were certainly a consideration but so was the political attempt to Russify the Soviet Union. Similar political factors behind urban diversity may be found in Romania and the former

Yugoslavia. Whilst emphasising the post-1945 dimension of urban diversity, it should not be forgotten that the cities of Europe have long been characterized by heterogeneity and greater or lesser degrees of cosmopolitanism as in Venice, Thessalonika or Antwerp in the sixteenth century for instance.

## National Diversity in Western Europe

France, perhaps the home of nationalism and for some the embodiment of the 'nation state' and certainly of 'the nation in arms', has in fact a vast range of national diversity. In the north there are Dutch speakers and in the east Germans, in the southeast Savoyards and Italians. Bretons and Corsicans aspire to linguistic distinctiveness (Marshall 1999), and in some cases political autonomy (Codaccioni, 1998). In the *Pays d'Oc*, Occitan, Catalan and Basque are regaining importance as both languages and national affiliations and identities. Modern France is the product of conquest, dynastic succession and accession. The nationalities within its borders partly reflect the machinations or military triumphs of Richelieu, Louis XIV or Napoleon III. Some of the nations, such as Brittany, are specific to France (though Brittany has historical, linguistic and cultural connections with Wales); some, such as the Germans, are the dominant nation in other states. Others, such as the Basques and Catalans, are nations spread across two states: in both these cases France and Spain.

This pattern of national diversity is frequent in states in Western Europe. The United Kingdom is made up of four nations. Scotland, one of these nations, has a distinct language of Scots, spoken predominantly in the lowlands. In the Highlands and Western Isles (and also, as a result of migration, in Glasgow) Gaelic is widely spoken and embodies a distinct lifestyle and culture. Welsh is now a compulsory subject in all schools in Wales. In the constitutionally unusual case of the Channel Islands, French is the predominant language. The partial revitalization of Manx and Cornish points to yet further self-conscious heterogeneity. Between Scotland and England there are important religious differences, reflecting the different historical pattern taken by the Reformation in what were, at that time, two separate kingdoms. A parliament for Scotland and assembly for Wales (there is a subtle difference) are political manifestations of the increasing importance and self-consciousness of nationality in the United Kingdom. Less politically interpreted as regionalism, this may be seen to be a trans-European trend (Harvie 1994).

Similarly in Spain the distinctiveness of the Basque country, Galicia and Catalonia is recognised by high levels of regional autonomy. Andalusia, Leon and Aragon exemplify further levels of diversity. It now seems that the high levels of autonomy that characterize Gallicia, the Basque country and Catalonia will be the pattern for all the autonomous regions that make up Spain. Language is again an important manifestation and symbol of these nationalities: about a quarter of the population speak a national language in addition to or, indeed, instead of Castilian Spanish. Catalan is the native language of six and a half million people: as such it is a larger entity than some of the official languages of the EU, such as Danish or Finnish. Castilian speakers in the Basque country have persevered in learning Basque. Language is not the only manifestation of national distinctiveness: cultural differences and distinct historical experiences are also important (Carr 1980; Hooper 1995). During the Franco era, the speaking of Catalan, for instance, was actively discouraged in favour of the Castilian of Madrid. When the Boulevard of the Generalissimo, in Barcelona, became the Boulevard of Catalonia, the language as well as the ideological orientation of the street sign was transformed. The suppressed, family language of Catalan broke free into vigorous civic life. In most of Catalonia now street signs and directions are not given in Spanish and Catalan but exclusively in the latter. In Spain, as in most European countries, this linguistic diversity has profound educational implications, which are considered later in this chapter.

Germany, re-united and with its capital returned to imperial Berlin, again may superficially appear to be an homogenous state. In fact there are Danes in the north in Schleswig Holstein (just as there are Germans in the south of Denmark) as well as Friesians and Sorbs, a Slavonic minority dispersed in the southeast (Bryant 1997; Jarausch 1997). Furthermore, Germans provide one of Europe's best examples of a dispersed nation. There are German minorities in Poland and all three Baltic States. The Gothic cities of Transylvania, such as Sibiu, date back to centuries-old settlements and provide an additional layer of diversity to that region. German families and communities are found as far east as Russia. Interestingly, these dispersed Germans have the right of citizenship in the Federal Republic. Under the communist regimes and also since then, following the widespread poverty brought about by economic liberalization, many made their way 'back' to Germany. The 'back' is in scare quotes because many of these families had left Germany over five hundred years ago and a significant number of them could not speak German. Many of these, from Russia, the Ukraine and Byelorussia, were German only in the sense of ethnic identity and through the nationality entry on the old Soviet passport. Reforms to the citizenship laws of Germany are under way, but nationality in Germany is currently defined not by place of birth or by language but by 'blood'.

In Italy national linguistic diversity is widely acknowledged. Richards, 1994 (though this text is not without racist overtones) itemises these as:

> Provencal French (in Valle d'Aosta and Turin); Friulano (in Gorizia and Udine, in the north-east); Ladino (in Bolzano and Trento); Occitano (in Turin and Cosenza); Sard (in Sardinia); Slovene (in Trieste, Gorizia and Udine); German (in Bolzano and elsewhere in the North); Albanian (in Palermo, Foggia and other places where Albanian communities had settled

in the past centuries); Catalan (in Sassari); Croatian (in Campobasso); and Greek (in Lecce, near Homer's birthplace, and Reggio Calabria).

(Richards 1995: 106)

This list does not include the substantial German-speaking, majority population of the South Tyrol (Fernandez-Armesto 1997). This last reference, covering the whole of Europe, is an invaluable resource for revealing the continent's astonishing national diversity.

Finland has a significant Swedish minority, geographically concentrated in the southwest and particularly in the Aland Islands. Since independence from Russia, the autonomy and civil rights granted to this minority (which has always been well linked into the Helsinki elite) have been an example of enlightenment for the whole continent (Kallio 1994). Of course, Finland also has Saami minorities in the far north and, increasingly, in the southern cities. Until recently there was considerably less to boast about in terms of support for their national distinctiveness. Sammi people speak a variety of connected languages. They are found in the north of Norway, Sweden, Finland and Russia and increasingly in the cities of southern Scandinavia.

The national diversity of Belgium is better known. French (Walloon) speakers are found in the south and Dutch speakers in the north (Flanders). Brussels is a city where both languages are found and acknowledged. In the south east there is also a small, politically recognized German community. The binding force for this linguistic diversity was, in the past, religion. Flanders and Wallonia remained Catholic and did not succeed in freeing themselves from their Spanish and Hapsburg dynasties. Thus although Flanders shared a language with the United Provinces to the north, this was less important in terms of national self-consciousness in the sixteenth and seventeenth centuries than religious and dynastic affiliation (Israel 1995). In the twentieth century language seems to have become the most important component of nationality and there is, not only in the xenophobic Vlaams Bloc, an increasing consciousness of links between Flanders and the Netherlands as well as some northern hostility towards Francophones (Hazecamp and Popple 1997).

The significant national minority in the Netherlands is the Friesians, who are also found along the eastern seaboard of Germany (European Bureau for Lesser Used Languages 1996). Geographically concentrated in the north-east and on the islands of the Waddenzee, they struggle to maintain their separate language. With their rural economy and picturesque costumes and festivals, they provide, like the Bretons or Scottish highlanders, an example of a national minority all too readily placed in an ethnic folklore museum by tourists and urban neighbours. The area round Groningen in the north, though united with the rest of the Netherlands in terms of language, maintains a strong sense of historical distinctiveness, regional identity and autonomy.

Greece is another state that maintains for its (Greek) citizens the illusion of homogeneity (Pollis 1992; Tsoucalas 1993). Given the historical emergence of the modern Greek state this is something of a triumph of wishful thinking. In the population exchange following the Greek disaster in Smyrna/Izmir in 1923, many of the people who came to Athens, Thessalonika and Patras were Turkish in their habits, their cuisine and frequently their language (Clogg 1992). It was chiefly their Orthodox religion that defined them as Greek. Even after the population exchange a sizeable Turkish minority remained in the north-eastern state of Thrace. This minority has significant civil rights, conceded as part of the settlement with Turkey. This is not the case for other national minorities, located particularly in the north but also increasingly in urban areas, Athens as well as Ioannina. Albanians formed a significant national presence in North-East Greece that the recent flood of refugees has only augmented. Vlachs are a minority (previously sponsored by the government of Romania that regarded them as linguistically related) whose civil and linguistic rights seem to be increasingly denied and eroded.

It is the combination of language and religion that gives such homogeneity to Greek ethnic identity. The illusion is that:

- all Greeks speak Greek
- only Greeks speak Greek
- all Greek are Greek Orthodox
- only Greeks are Greek Orthodox (though related religions are obviously recognized).

This conflation of language and religion into one exclusive national identity is exceedingly powerful. However, it fails to recognize the demographic diversity of Greece in either linguistic or religious terms (Georgiadou 1995; Karaflogka 1997).

The Greeks, like the Germans, provide a rich example of a diaspora (or dispersed nation). In both cases this is global rather than purely European. There are large Greek populations in the United States and Australia. A much-cited example gives Melbourne and not Thessalonika as the second largest Greek urban community. Parts of the remaining Greek diaspora in Europe date back to settlement that took place more than two millennia ago (Ascherson 1996). In southern Italy, on the Black Sea coasts of Bulgaria and northern Turkey, there are still components of the Greek community. Before the 1923 disaster there were more Greek speakers in Smyrna than in Athens. The Greek presence in Cavafy's city of Alexandria is today less prominent even than at the time of Durrell's evocation. More recent migrations have taken Greeks in search of work and fortune to the cities of Switzerland, Germany and the Netherlands, and Greek Cypriots predominantly to London (see the discussion on urban diversity later in this chapter).

The Jews are another diaspora widely dispersed across east and west Europe. Some areas of concentration remain in London or Manchester. Others, such as those in Thessalonika or Vilnius, effectively disappeared with the Holocaust. Some, like Antwerp, are gradually being re-established. With the disappearance of Yiddish, it is religious affiliation which continues to hold this community together (Bash 1998); it is also increasingly a matter of political solidarity in the aftermath of the Holocaust, which in some cases centres on a commitment to the state of Israel. In all cases, New York, southern California and especially Israel seem to offer more attractive, safer havens than Europe. While distinctive Jewish schooling is perhaps only an issue in the United Kingdom, the curricular treatment of the Holocaust at all levels remains a major challenge to all European education systems (Supple 1993).

## National Diversity in Eastern Europe

Perhaps it was the wars in former Yugoslavia that brought home to the west that in the east of Europe difference is different. National diversity is more widespread, involves political and religious as well as linguistic loyalties and, above all, can be exceptionally fiercely held. Or is this generalization itself a lapse into stereotypes? Into a spurious and unnecessary distinction between east and west?

While elements of this generalization can be substantiated, it is necessary to remember that east and west Europe are themselves political constructs, products in particular of cold war ideology. The Iron Curtain marked the line made in the Yalta deal between Stalin, Roosevelt and Churchill as much as the limits of penetration of the various armies at the end of the Second World War. Thus Greece and Finland were in the political west, and subsequently members of its embodiment the European Union, while Slovenia, geographically further west, was in the political east. As the Iron Curtain became both taken for granted and the boundary of political and military hostility, older and possibly more enduring patterns of European organization – the Hapsburg Empire, a self-conscious central Europe, the Baltic, the Adriatic – were forgotten. As political repression and economic austerity came to be contrasted with the (would that it were) free and prosperous west, the European heritage of Riga, Cracow and Prague, the inter-war cosmopolitanism of Bucharest, were too easily forgotten. Northern Greece was the west, Yugoslavian Macedonia the east. The continuation of this discourse should then be used with some caution and with a recollection of longitudinal accuracy.

To return to the generalization concerning fiercely held political and religious difference, it would actually be as easy to point to these elements in the conflict in Ireland as in Yugoslavia. Indeed the language element of the conflict is less important in the western case than in the 'east'. Language, although an element in the politicization of independence in the state of Ireland, was not an important

31

component of the Troubles. The differences between the communities in Northern Ireland are attributed to religion, though they have long been codified by history and folklore into patriotic song and Orange marches. The murderous bombing of civilian targets in both Northern Ireland and England, as well as sectarian killings and political assassinations, cannot but manifest the fierceness of this conflict. The sometimes overwhelming presence of the British army reveals its full military nature. Certainly Ireland, after independence, avoided any full-scale military conflict such as has occurred, and may well occur again, in former Yugoslavia. Furthermore, in Yugoslavia linguistic and even calligraphic difference impacted on religious diversity to give the complex cartography of intersecting hostilities. Nevertheless, any polarity between the civilized, peaceful west and the nationalistic and warlike east is utterly to be avoided.

Romania has three regions: Wallachia, Moldavia and Transylvania. Until 1918 Transylvania was part of the Austro-Hungarian Empire. Cities such as Cluj or Oradea have inherited civic centres of Hapsburg elegance. As part of Austro-Hungary the official language was Hungarian, though Romanian was also spoken. As noted earlier, German was and still is spoken in the Gothic cities and elsewhere. The German population has declined through movement to Germany but is still strong. Romanian became the language of the region when it was incorporated in that state. In Transylvania, as in the rest of Romania and also Bulgaria, Hungary and Slovakia, there are many gypsy or Roma people with their distinct Roma languages. The Romanian people, in so far as they maintain a religious orientation after the years of communism, are Greek Orthodox Christians. The Hungarians, or Magyars, are mainly Catholic but sometimes Protestant. It is not uncommon in even quite small towns to see two churches, sometimes side by side, and occasionally almost identical on the outside. This then is an area where national diversity is complex and carries deep historical residues (Fischer-Galati 1991; Murphy 1992; Rady 1992; Rich 1998a). Romanian governments have encouraged the migration of Romanians from Wallachia and Moldavia to Transylvania as part of a process of Romanianization. This process was particularly intense under the Ceaucescu regime when an attempt was also made to eradicate the Hungarian villages. There are ethnic conflicts at local level between Magyars and Romanians and between both these groups and the Roma. At a national level this is manifested by the polarization of political parties along 'ethnic', that is nationality, lines. Not surprisingly, education is one of the main areas of political conflict between these groups.

Hungary is very conscious of the treatment of Magyar minorities, not only in Transylvania which contains the most significant of these, but also in Slovakia, Croatia and Serbia (especially Vojvodina). Thus the Magyar people and politicians of Transylvania can call upon support from the government across the border. Needless to say, this is hardly a popular ploy with Romanian nationalists. Where a minority in one state is actually a majority in control of a state elsewhere, it may actually be in a more powerful position in relation to its own majority state.

Again the Ireland analogy holds, but this could also be applied to Quebec or Latvia (as discussed later). Magyars in Transylvania have certainly looked at the relative economic success across the border with some envy. They can, furthermore, point to the apparently preferential way in which the Hungarian government treats its Romanian minority (Hungarian Ministry of Culture and Communication 1995; Ministry of Culture and Education (Hungary) 1995). Although currently there is a delicate agreement between Budapest and Bucharest on the treatment of minorities, it is possible that the different accession dates to the European Union and NATO may exacerbate tension and conflict.

Latvia is a state where conflict between nationalities has been, and in some respects still is, so intense that even demographic data, particularly those that apply to the past, are unreliable (see for instance Dreifelds 1996; Lieven 1993; Stamers 1993; UNDP 1995). The inter-war, independent state of Latvia was composed of many nationalities. Latvians predominated, but there were also many Russians as well as Germans, Poles, Lithuanians, Ukrainians, Jews and Byelorussians, The Jews were destroyed not only by the German Holocaust but by local and Soviet hostility (again reliable facts here are not easy to come by). During the Soviet period many Latvians were deported to central Asia and Siberia, and many Russians moved or were moved into the Latvian cities (thus leading to urban diversity on top of the existing national diversity). In a sense, what Latvia has is national diversity compounded by urban diversity. The result is a high level of demographic fracture and the potential for tension. Leaving aside the other minorities, almost half of the population is Russian, and a similar proportion Latvian. In the cities the Russians are in the majority, slight in Riga but substantial in the second city, Daugavpils. In the period after the regained independence of 1991, the Latvians regarded the Russians as the Soviet usurpers of their liberty and as the people who brought their nation to the brink of extinction. The Russians, formerly the dominant group, now find themselves disenfranchised and, as a group at least, disliked. The Russians in Latvia, like the Magyars in Transylvania, are one of those groups that can turn to a state across the border controlled by their group. Russia, even in temporary decline, is exceptionally powerful. Education and citizenship in Latvia are considered in Chapter Four.

## Theorizing Difference

Another parenthesis is necessary at this point, in order to clarify the terms in which these debates are characteristically conducted. For the Latvians in Latvia, the Romanians in Transylvania or, for that matter, the Welsh in Wales or London, what they see themselves as constituting is a nation, a race or an ethnic group. Social scientists, more frequently observers than participants in group conflict, may use the term nation, though often in real or implied scare quotes. They are, however, exceedingly reluctant to use terms like race and ethnic group. There are two main reasons for this. First, the terms lack precision. The biological theories of race have long been discredited. How then can one rationally determine to what race or ethnic group someone belongs? There are relatively objective answers to this: one can note what language a group of people speak, what their religion is, in what region(s) they are located, what their cultural practices are in terms of diet, family organization, ritual and so forth. One can even ask people to what group they perceive themselves as belonging, thereby confirming their self-ascribed ethnicity. But less objective factors also come into play: appearance, skin colour, perceptions of 'us' and 'them'. This leads to the second reason for eschewing the discourse of race or ethnicity: not only does it all too readily lead to a racist lexicon, it is actually derived from theories and research which are largely based on racist premises. Much writing on cultural and social studies is unfortunately derived from just these premises: Young emphasizes the extent of their permeation: 'Race became the fundamental determinant of human culture and history: indeed it is arguable that race became *the* common principle of academic knowledge in the nineteenth century' (Young 1995a: 93).

In choosing to stay firmly within the terminology of language, religion and culture, it is necessary to recognize, first, that there is frequently considerable overlap between these categories and, second, that the group cohesions which they maintain and reproduce in European society can be exceedingly strong. (The example of Greece was described earlier.) It is the strength of these cohesions that can continue to take social scientists and politicians by surprise.

> Culture has always marked cultural difference by producing the other; it has always been comparative, and racism has always been an integral part of it: the two are inextricably clustered together, feeding off and generating each other. Race has always been culturally constructed. Culture has always been racially constructed.
>
> (Young 1995a: 54)

For people ranging from Northern Irish Protestants to Serbs in Belgrade, these factors of group cohesion, and of course of exclusion, form one of the principle motives of belief and behaviour. For such peoples the difference between catholic and protestant is not 'simply' one of religion: it involves family and group history, tradition, daily transactions and solidarities, economic and political choices and behaviours. It is the organizing principle of individual and group identity. School and university knowledge are not separate from this process or secondary to it. They are intrinsic to its fierce maintenance and reproduction. In Northern Ireland, for instance, there are at least six private, all-age schools run by Protestant groups where the theory of evolution is only taught so that it can be rigorously rebutted by biblical texts. The nature of the school knowledge and the nature of the community are mutually self-supporting (Byrne and Mckeown 1998).

In order to deal with the strength of affiliation to such communities, social sciences use the term *ethnic identity*. Thus while there might be no such thing as an ethnic group, there can be a group which holds a perceived ethnic identity. This concept allows the recognition of the various groups in Europe who define themselves in terms of nationality or ethnicity. It also recognizes the strength of these affiliations, that for some groups and individuals issues concerning their language, religion or group loyalties are essential to the structuring of their identities. It is then possible to talk of ethnic identity as well as language, religion and culture, without lapsing into racist theories of ethnicity.

Ethnic and national identity in Europe is conflicted. The highly complex demographic distribution of difference is a challenge to the European cartographer. But it is anyway not a static map. Groups continue to be in conflict for territory and political power. As indicated earlier, ethnic identities are often forged in contradistinction to others and to out-groups. Would Northern Irish Protestants be able to maintain the strength of their internal solidarity if there were no Catholics? Political parties based on ethnic identity formalize these conflicts in Northern Ireland and Romania. In former Yugoslavia these forms of solidarity have led to civil war and genocide.

## Education and National Diversity: Introducing the Issues

In educational terms these conflicts are frequently over the control of schooling and universities – the Romanianization of the university of Cluj or the use of Dutch at the Catholic University of Leuven in Belgium with the associated foundation of the new University of Louvain – and over the content of the school and university curricula. In terms of content, two subjects are frequently the areas of highest conflict: history and language. In Europe, the joke has it, states go to war not to control the future but to control the past. The history curriculum of states is dictated by the victors, as was clear in the schools and universities of Eastern Europe between 1945 and 1989, and in Japan too in the post-war period. Internal victors can make similar changes, as the Greek colonels did in stressing traditional, classical and Orthodox aspects of the school curriculum up to 1974. In other countries, such as Northern Ireland or Spain, different versions of the state's history may be taught in different schools and universities. In the Irish case this will vary according to the religious denomination of the institution; in the Spanish case the variation will be more by geographical region (Mackey 1997). History is the main subject in which the state, as in France, attempts to disguise itself as the nation. In most European countries the formation, liberation or unification of the state-disguised-as-nation forms the major theme of school and university history. In all European countries the importance of the individual state to world history will be exaggerated. In few countries are unsavoury episodes from the state's past – the slave trade in the United Kingdom, the Inquisition in Spain, the Holocaust in Germany – given a great deal of attention.

Conflicts over the language curricula of schools and universities take many forms in Europe, and these conflicts are themes in several of the succeeding chapters. Perhaps the most notable, and certainly the one where conflict is at its most intense, concerns asymmetric bilingualism. This occurs where more than one language is spoken in a region and one of the language-groups either forms a significant majority of the population or has control of the central state or both. Wales, Transylvania and Catalonia provide contrasting examples of state policy towards asymmetric bilingualism. In Wales, Welsh is the language of the home in areas of the north and west. Westminster state policy towards Welsh asymmetric bilingualism has adapted over the years. During the nineteenth century there was a concerted campaign to eliminate the Welsh language, in which the English-speaking school system was an important instrument. Welsh, unlike Cornish, survived this pressure and the state now attempts to encourage the Welsh language both in education and the media. Now Welsh-speaking schools have become popular in the south as well as the north, partly through their perceived high standards as well as parents' linguistic nationalism (Welsh Office 1995). Many subjects can be studied to degree level in Welsh at the University of Wales. As mentioned above, even English-speaking pupils in Wales must learn some Welsh even in those schools where English is the language of instruction. This is all within limits, of course: although government offices in Wales must respond to people in English or Welsh, according to their expressed preference, Welsh still cannot be spoken on the floor of the House of Commons. Furthermore, it would be exceedingly difficult to find outside the Principality either classes taught in Welsh or, with a few exceptions in non-state provision, Welsh language lessons. Many English-speaking students compelled by the school curriculum to learn Welsh do so reluctantly, badly and with an ill grace. The tension between a centralizing curricular system and increasingly self-conscious cultural and linguistic diversity has been uneasily resolved in Wales. The establishment of the Welsh Assembly may provide further opportunities for the Welsh language to spread and thrive.

In Transylvania there are four main languages: Romanian, Hungarian, German and Roma. The latter receives virtually no official recognition within the education system or the other bodies of the state (McDonald 1999). The other three languages retain a level of equality at least at the school level. There are separate Romanian-speaking, German-speaking and Hungarian-speaking schools at primary and secondary levels. Where the bipartite system exists there are Hungarian and German grammar schools as well as those operating in Romanian. Again German-speaking schools, though not Hungarian, are popular with middle-class Romanian-speaking parents because of their perceived high standards. Where there are no places available in Hungarian-speaking schools, the education and particularly the language maintenance of Hungarian-speaking pupils is less well maintained. Conflict in Transylvania is about university level education, which has already been mentioned, and about the content of the curricula, particularly those concerning history and geography (Rich 1998a, 1998b). Here central government insistence that these subjects be taught in Romanian, or at least using Romanian terminology, place names and bias has led to political conflict in Bucharest itself.

In Wales, Welsh is not the language of the urbanized south. By contrast Catalan is spoken in Barcelona, one of Europe's large cities. Thus, although similar attempts were made in the past, especially under the Franco dictatorship, to eliminate Catalan and impose Castilian, they have been doomed to failure. Catalan was the language of Barcelona and of Catalonia's resistance to both Franco and the associated Castilian. With the restoration of democracy and the high level of regional autonomy in Spain, Catalan has returned as the language of instruction in many schools and to university level at the *Autonoma*. The non-Catalan-speaking inhabitants of Barcelona (migrants to the prosperous Barcelona from other parts of Spain) make a contrast with many of the English speakers in Wales. Not only are they willing that there children should be educated in Catalan, they are keen to learn it themselves (Hooper 1995).

## Urban Diversity in Western and Eastern Europe

At the start of this chapter, demographic diversity was broadly divided into two types: national diversity and urban diversity. Turning now to urban diversity, this term is intended to categorize that new – at least in terms of quantity – pattern of heterogeneity which has emerged in Europe since 1945 largely as the result of immigration into the expanding cities (King 1998). As urbanization has continued, people from rural areas have been attracted to the more favourable economic conditions, and sometimes more liberal political climate, which have existed in cities. In some cases this has led to movements within a state, as with the urbanization of Istanbul or Ankara; in others, it has led to international migration and settlement. In this respect the cities of Germany, Switzerland, the Netherlands, France and the United Kingdom have been particularly attractive.

In the west this immigration may be seen to have followed in reverse the lines of earlier imperialism:

- from the Indian subcontinent, the West Indies and East and West Africa to the cities of the United Kingdom
- from the Moluccas and Surinam to those of the Netherlands
- from Indo-China and the Maghreb to France

- from Anatolia (never a colony, of course, but an area of previous intense, economic and political interest) to Germany
- from Libya and, as refugees, Ethiopia to Italy.

In addition people from the poorer regions of Europe, particularly the south but also the east (including, mainly, the former Democratic Republic) have flooded into the immensely rich cities of western Germany: Hamburg, Cologne, Stuttgart, Munich, Frankfort, Dussledorf and the western part of Berlin. This demographic movement has resulted in large populations in the western cities of 'immigrants', 'gastarbeiters', 'minorities', 'auslanders' or 'foreigners'. They form a sizeable proportion of the populations of cities such as Rotterdam, Birmingham, Copenhagen, Brussels, Marseilles and Hanover. In some cases these minorities are themselves exceedingly heterogeneous: to take the extreme example, there are probably over four hundred languages spoken by the children in the schools of London. In other cases there are concentrations of particular identifiable groups, such as Magrhebians in Lyons or Marseilles.

In eastern and central Europe, while there has been internal migration in the process of urbanization, specifically international migration to the cities is not a marked phenomenon. But the internal urban migration has had consequences for diversity. The state-assisted movement of workers from Wallachia and Moldavia to the cities of Transylvania was part of an attempt to Romanianize that region. The much larger movements of people, over many decades, within the former Soviet Union were an attempt at Russification. The mass expulsions and forced movements of people from national regions are well recorded, the Baltic States, Inguchetia, Chechnya, the Crimean Tartars, the Volga Germans. The group and individual tragedies that these movements entailed remain a potent force in the politics of the states of the former Soviet Union, from the Transcaucasus to the Baltic. Parallel to these deportations was the movement of Russian-speaking people into the cities of the Baltic area and other regions, either as workers or as military and security personnel. It is this process of Russification that has led to the ethnic politics in Lithuania and especially Moldova, Latvia and Estonia today. Education policy, in terms of language, itself played a major part in the policy of Russification across the former Soviet Union (Haarmann 1995; Khazanov 1995). In the case of the Baltic States, urban diversity reinforced national diversity by increasing the proportion of Russians within the main cities of these states. Daugavpils, the second city of Latvia, has a large Russian-speaking majority. It is easy here to confound national diversity with urban diversity and to assume that all the Russian speakers are the result of the process of Russification. This is an historical mistake: there were many Russian speakers in the Baltic States before the Molotov–Ribbentrop Pact illegally ceded them to Stalin. Before turning to education policy, then, it is important to underline the point that, while in the west urban diversity refers to the heterogeneous population of black, southern and often Islamic peoples, in the Baltic States and other areas of the former Soviet Union it refers predominantly to the presence of Russians.

The prevalence of urban diversity adds another level of complexity to issues of group cohesion and context and to the construction of individual identities. In terms of identity the overlap between national and urban diversity presents some difficulties. Do Bangladeshi speakers living and working in Cardiff consider themselves to be Bangladeshi, Welsh or British? It is likely that their self-perceptions vary: they will be Bangladeshi whilst at the mosque or a family meal; perhaps Welsh whilst playing or watching rugby and British – if at all – while voting in a general election, or on a visit to London. In these cases people may be seen to have multiple identities which alternate according to context. Following the 1998 referendum in Latvia and general election in Germany, it is likely that the large groups of non-citizens in these states will be able more readily to obtain citizenship. In cases such as these the formation of multiple identities is likely to become increasingly widespread. It will more easy to be both Russian and Latvian, both Turkish and German or Turkish and Bavarian.

## Diversity and Knowledge: Introducing the Issues

In terms of cultural and epistemological diversity, these urban groups both widen and deepen the patterns of difference. The presence of mosques, for instance, with their distinctive outline and minaret, embodies one of the different groups and forms of solidarity now common in western cities. Urban groups bring major religious belief systems into the cities of the west: Buddhism, Hinduism and Sikhism as well as Islam. Each of these religions has associated philosophies of what it is to be human, of the nature of society, of the relationship between humanity and the rest of the natural world, about how the material world can be best understood. They bring a wide diversity of languages, including major world tongues such as Hindi, Chinese, Bangladeshi, Turkish, Gujerati, Urdu, Arabic and Swahili. Again these languages, often in association with a particular religion, bring verbal cultures of literature, philosophy, history and science. These belief systems and cultures may be radically different from the traditional Protestant, Catholic or Orthodox Christianity of the cities of Western Europe. They are different too from the beliefs and practices of modernist society in terms of science, democracy and capitalism. They are also often fundamentally different from each other.

What is at issue here are different epistemologies, different versions of truth. To take Islam as an example, this is not only a religion with a set of beliefs and practices (Nielsen 1994; Parker-Jenkins 1991, 1994; Sarwar, 1984, 1993). It is also a way of organizing family life, of dividing labour between men and women and between children and adults. It carries with it dietary practices and various patterns of cuisine. It is associated with major strands in world literature and with various forms of non-representational artistic products. It has its own music and styles of architecture as well as its own litany. It carries with it a particular view and philosophy of history, with its own starting date, different from the Christian era common in Europe. It has a view of science not as the process of the discoveries of humanity but rather as the revelations of God. It can be associated with various forms of political and economic organization, but these are not automatically those of capitalism and democracy. Islam is not some traditionalistic, folklore backwater: it is an important way of understanding humanity, the natural world and society. It has a range of highly successful artistic traditions that go back for a millennium and half. It is a major force in current world politics from Sarajevo to Djakarta. It does not seek to be reconciled either with Christianity or with modernity.

Islam is only one of the important epistemologies and cultures now found in the cities of Western Europe. The existence of this epistemological plurality means that conflicts between groups in society can increasingly be about knowledge: the theory of evolution; the ethics of medical research; the Turkish conquest of Constantinople and the Balkans; international languages. In approaching differences and conflicts between the cultures and knowledge systems of different nationalities or different urban groups, it is essential, to lapse for the sake of clarity briefly into the normative, to retain some sense of cultural relativism. It is necessary to be exceedingly cautious of the view that the culture or knowledge system which one maintains oneself is necessarily superior to, or more true than, that held by other individuals and groups. Cultures and knowledge systems of other groups must not be regarded as subordinate, derivative, heretical, or folkloric: they must be granted integrity within the goodness, beauty and truth claims (or within non-Socratic terminology if such is their persuasion) which they make for themselves. Yet it is against this background of cultural and epistemological plurality and conflict, perhaps even because of this background, that the states of Europe are increasingly turning to centrally controlled curricular uniformity. The population of Europe has never been more diverse; this diversity is increasingly an important aspect of group and individual identity. Yet states are responding to this, through school and university curricular systems, by attempting to enforce homogenous paradigms of knowledge.

Ensuing chapters will go on to argue that within this fundamental tension are other contradictions no less important. With the development of the knowledge economy, knowledge itself is becoming increasingly internationalized. This also contrasts with curricular homogenization that so frequently has a national(ist) emphasis. Another way of understanding these processes is in terms of a society which is increasingly post industrial and associated with a cultural and episte-mological critique which conceptualises itself in terms of *postmodernity*, but is at odds with curricular systems that remain firmly *modernist* or indeed are relapsing towards *traditionalism*. It is in these terms that the argument is continued in the next chapter.

## Discussion Questions

1 The chapter insists that no state in Europe is a nation. Is this correct?
2 To what extent has language replaced religion as the most important element in national identification in Europe and the USA? If Northern Ireland and the former Yugoslavia are anomalous, why is this the case?
3 To what extent is the concept of ethnic identity an attempt to reintroduce 'race' into the discourse of social sciences by the back door?
4 Should schools and universities teach about the Holocaust? How should this topic be treated?
5 Are there any ways in which it is possible to arbitrate between the different epistemologies of different groups?

## Further Reading

The distinction between states and nations is powerfully made by Appadurai (1990) 'Disjuncture and Difference in the Global Cultural Economy', in M. Featherstone (ed.), *Global Culture: Nationalism, Globalisation and Modernity*. London: Sage. His widely referenced article makes clear the ways in which the state and the nation are each other's project.

Readers interested in national diversity in Europe could consult the publications of The European Bureau for Lesser Used Languages. For an up to date account of urban diversity in Europe see the contributions in: Pinder, D. (ed.) (1998) *The New Europe: Economy, Society and Environment*. Chichester: John Wiley.

For exhaustive information and analysis of urban and national diversity in the United States, reference should be made to Banks, J. A. and Banks, C. A. M. (1995) *Handbook of Research on Multicultural Education*. New York: Macmillan.

# 4 The Creation and Re-Creation of Tradition in Schools and Universities

## Traditional Elements in the Curriculum

This chapter considers the importance of tradition in the curricula of European schools and universities. It does this in three ways.

- First, it considers in what, in the different countries of Europe, the traditional consists.
- Second, it draws a distinction between traditional, modern and postmodern conceptions of curriculum formation.
- Third, it exemplifies the creation and recreation of tradition in various curricular systems.

Because schools and, especially, universities are so closely associated with and so deeply implicated in the enlightenment project, it is sometimes difficult to recall that their origin and their appeal are more frequently to more traditional roots. The following elements of school and university curricula are here identified as derived from, or appealing to, traditional values, beliefs and practices. Although separated here, for purposes of clarity, they are in practice, closely interlinked:

- religious instruction, denominational teaching and acts of collective worship
- a stress on particular social forms, especially those of the nuclear or extended family and the procedures and beliefs necessary to uphold these; the reproduction of gendered identities and expectations
- the encouragement of certain forms of embodiment which may stress health or fitness or discipline and which validate participation in certain leisure activities while strongly discouraging others
- the practices of social control within schools and universities themselves and the inculcation of the norms of wider control for the purposes of stratified social reproduction; the practices of surveillance and evaluation
- the legitimation of the state's monopoly of violence not only as a mode of

control but also as an internalization of national or 'ethnic' identity; the construction of individuality within the political doctrines of the state

- the reproduction of tradition itself, in forms concerning the importance of particular narratives of history and the impact of these on current modes of legitimation and identity formation
- the stress on Europe as the cradle of human culture and civilization, which may be stressed in political, scientific, artistic, philosophical, technological or even military dimensions; the perceived virtues of Roman, and particularly Hellenic, structures and products may be emphasized.

Before proceeding to scrutinize each of these points in turn, it is worth noting that with the last of them one of the central concerns of this book has been reached: the importance in Europe as a whole of the concept of Europe itself in the production and reproduction of tradition.

## Religion

It is almost impossible to overstate the importance of religious institutions and beliefs – overwhelmingly but not exclusively Christian – in the formation and structure of European education systems. In at least two countries, Norway and Greece, education and religion are administered by the same government departments. In Greece only Orthodox Christians are allowed to become teachers in mainstream schools (Georgiadou 1995). In Ireland too education and religion are closely linked at government level. Religious institutions retain control of schools in countries as different as Italy, the Netherlands and England and Wales. A sixth of all schools in Spain are run by religious orders or groups (Hooper 1995). Universities are controlled by religious institutions in, for instance, Belgium, Spain and Romania. Management and control by no means charts the limits of the influence of religious institutions on European curricular systems. This influence was almost ubiquitous – the anomalous case of France needs to be considered – in the European Union countries, Switzerland and Norway, and is re-emerging in those states formally under direct or indirect Soviet control. This re-emergence is both internally and externally directed: internally as in the return of Catholic elements to Polish schooling, or externally as in the creation of Baptist universities in Romania. 'In Turkmenistan the history of Islam has been included into the high school curriculum by presidential decree' (Khazanov 1995: 145). Despite the importance of religion, however, it remains a terrain of conflict, compromise and accommodation within European curricular systems.

There are some common features of religious influence on European curricular systems. In the many countries where religion is explicitly taught in primary and secondary schools, it is almost always Christianity. There may be some nodding acknowledgement of demographic cultural plurality, there may be some – usually tokenistic – concessions to multiculturalism, but the stories told, the festivals celebrated, the beliefs endorsed and promulgated, the hymns and prayers chanted will be predominantly those of Christianity. In those states and institutions where the link with particular churches is explicit – the Catholic University of Leuven, say or Church of England voluntary-aided primary schools – there is institutional interpenetration between education and religion. The symbols, spaces, rituals and personnel of the church form part of the structuration of the school or university. Similarly the activities and personnel of the school are visible and explicit in the space of the church or cathedral: cultural productions of the B Minor Mass, endearing nativity plays by the infants, exhibitions of pupils' writing and artwork, and so on. In this way children and young people's very notion of what it is to be educated is inscribed within the particular beliefs, behaviours and knowledges of Christianity. In some ways the explicit religious teaching may actually be less important than this wider context of cultural inscription. To the extent that religious teaching is designed to reproduce fervent Christian beliefs among the citizens of Europe, it has been remarkably unsuccessful. But in terms of the legitimation of a set of values and versions of history and tradition, in the reproduction of certain mental categories – virtue, family, respect, continuity, authority – it may have performed far more effectively.

A further common element, though more often associated with Protestantism than Catholicism, is the focus upon a text. Biblical exegesis is the antecedent of much European scholarly activity. Respect for the text, and even the rigorous pleasures of hermeneutics associated with postmodernism, have emerged from this tradition of intellectual activity. With classicism, the other main source of these procedures, Christianity long ago made its accommodation. In European curricular systems, classical values and those of Christianity are rarely portrayed as being in opposition. (Matthew Arnold may have essayed this, but much more characteristic are curricular systems such as that of Greece where Byzantium provides the bridge between Hellenic civilization and that of orthodoxy.) The Aquinan solution of making classicism and Christianity an unproblematic continuation has prevailed: Rome and Catholicism are conflated, and within curricular systems all elements of perceived classical Athenian life are valued and approved apart from the belief system.

Christianity in Europe, of course, is by no means unitary. The contrary remains fiercely the case and religious education and forms of worship in school may be strongly sectarian. In some states one form of Christianity predominates and the sectarian teaching, in Ireland or the Netherlands for example, follows from this. In some countries such as Belgium or Northern Ireland there is effectively a bipartite schooling system, with state or Protestant Christianity influencing one sector and Catholicism controlling another. In Northern Ireland, as has been mentioned in the preceding chapter, this reaches oppositional dimensions with the state-funded Catholic schools and the state-funded Protestant schools teaching not only different versions of Christianity but also opposing versions of history, culture and politics (Byrne and Mckeown 1998). Beyond this there are the privately-funded Protestant schools teaching an even more extreme and oppositional curriculum. Parallel situations can be noted in other divided societies, notably Bosnia-Hercegovina.

Non-Christian religions are, of course, represented inside European curricular systems. In England and Wales there have been for many years state-funded Jewish primary and secondary schools. With the departure of the vigorously anti-pluralist Conservative government this tolerance is now being extended to Islamic schools (Lepkowska 1998). The decades of conflict that have been necessary to achieve this recognition are testament to the strength of Christian, traditional forces within the education system of England and Wales. Conflict and compromise better characterize this system than any notions of hegemony. Nevertheless, religious pluralism in education is a difficult aim to achieve in the protestant parts of Germany as well as in catholic Ireland and orthodox Greece. But historical pluralism – the Jewish university of Vilnius, say, destroyed in the Holocaust – and present day tolerance both point to the possibility of religious coexistence. The fragile state of Bosnia-Hercegovina is currently divided into two parts. Neither tolerance nor pluralism could be said to characterize Republika Srpska. The other part, the Muslim–Croat federation, currently manifests a degree of curricular fragmentation (Buchan 1998; Done 1998). Nevertheless in Sarajevo and the other Muslim areas, the presence of Islam in the curriculum has a geographical identity in Europe.

Perhaps the most remarkable of religion's curricular compromises has been that with modernity. Among many other conflicts, the French revolution was a contest between tradition and modernity. In terms of the school curriculum this conflict was resolved in favour of the modern. Religion is not taught in French state schools, which maintain an ethos of muscular secularity. Republicanism and the laity form the centre of this ethos. This can lead to conflict with traditional religious groups, both Christian and Islamic. In the latter case the defenders of the laity can be seen to be the enemies of cultural tolerance when conflicts arise over the wearing of religious costume or symbols in school. Interestingly, non-secular schooling was one of the products of the revolution that France did not succeed in exporting. Elsewhere the conflict between tradition and modernity in the nineteenth century – over geological evidence, say, or the theory of evolution – led to a compromise that persists in many places today. The compromise allows science to teach its version of truth whilst religion teaches another, with neither schools nor universities, with their entrenched departments of theology, attempting to make any definitive arbitration between them.

## The Family and the Body

Civics lessons, home economics, tutorial work and assemblies as well as religious education and acts of worship all play a part in producing and reproducing patterns of social interaction. In the schools and universities of Europe these patterns range from ones of authority and deference in some systems to those that aim for mutual recognition and respect between, for example, children and young people on the one hand and adults on the other. In all, however, there are implicit and/or explicit emphases on certain forms of social formation and certain patterns of division of responsibility, labour and reward. To say that European schools stress the centrality of the workplace and the family is almost to state the self-evident. Yet the nature of the family inscribed on the content of schooling differs from one state to another, being more nuclear in the Netherlands or the United Kingdom, and more extended and inter-generational in Greece or Poland. Similarly the simplified, hierarchical workplace of an English secondary technology lesson is very different from the complex, multifaceted workplace of the German apprenticeship scheme.

The family and the gendered division of labour traditionally associated with it are not merely exemplified in curricular content – marriage as the resolution of conflict in Shakespeare's comedies or Jane Austen's novels – they are manifested in the structure of educational establishments themselves. The distinction between adult and child, the proper modes of costume, deportment and address, the internalization of authority structures into the language of deference are all ways in which schools replicate, or indeed exaggerate, the structures of the family. Similarly the gender division of authority embodied in the traditional family is all too often repeated in schools and universities. The Greek example (Kontogiannopoulou-Polydories and Zambeta 1997) provides an extreme version of a pattern found across Europe of men being overwhelmingly represented in senior positions in schools and universities, and women equally prevalent at the lower and more marginal levels. Headteachers and professors are disproportionately men; teachers, ancillaries, part-time lecturers are disproportionately women. The actual structures of schools and universities teach pupils and students the legitimacy of gendered hierarchies, and inevitably lead both boys and girls to construct identities and to adjust expectations accordingly.

The neglected area of the role of the school and university curricula in the creation of special educational needs and disability is dealt with in detail in Chapter Six. The all too frequent exclusion from mainstream schools of children perceived to have special needs reveals the constrained expectations of human behaviour and appearance, the normative nature of educational embodiment. Biology lessons, home economics and other technology subjects, and physical education all stress European ideals of health and fitness (and more covertly beauty and strength). Again, these norms and aspirations are strongly gendered, with boys and young men still likely to study different areas of technology as well as participate in completely different sports (woodwork, metalwork, computers, football, rugby, basketball) from girls and young women (cookery, fabrics, hockey, netball, gymnastics, dance).

The status of particular areas of study within the still subject-organized school and university curriculum interacts with gendered expectations in the family and the workplace. Subjects at which boys and young men excel – mathematics, physical sciences, information and communications technology (ICT) and, in the north west, medicine – are granted high status within education systems, unlike the subjects more associated with female success – such as languages and humanities. Not surprisingly there is a high correlation between high-status male subjects and those areas of expertise that can command remuneration and status in the workplace. In Russia medicine is a much more predominantly female profession and accordingly is attributed less status and reward than in the west. As middle-class young women proceed to be doctors and lawyers, in the UK, Greece and France for instance, the gender aspect of subject status may be partially undermined. However, these women represent only a small section of the population. Furthermore, some subjects such as ICT seem to be increasingly rather than decreasingly gendered; and, even if the gender aspect is partially undermined, the hierarchical organization of subject status remains.

The cult of normality, fitness and health in the curricula of European schools and universities is related to wider patterns of production and consumption. The teaching of football, to take a prime example, in schools and universities is obviously not unconnected either to the multi-million European soccer industry or to the significant beer sales in cities on Saturday afternoons. Whilst the creation of the alcohol guzzling male sporting identity is encouraged both in universities and in the senior years of schools, other forms of recreational drug use are actively discouraged. The health and pastoral curricula of countries such as Denmark or Scotland explicitly address the perceived evils of many drugs, from cocaine, through ecstasy to nicotine. Similarly, traditional curricula emphasize the pleasures of the concert hall rather than those of the disco. Teenage sexual activity is discouraged by the school and university curriculum either explicitly or implicitly through the work load it places on those pupils and students who are determined to succeed. The great dissonance between the pleasures of youth culture and the austerities of the curriculum are one of the reasons why such a colossal exercise in identity control as the education system can be seen to be only partially successful. Intellectual athleticism and solvent-abusing hedonism form the polarities of youth identity formation in Europe. Where an individual locates on this polarity is dependent on social class and the related compliance with the school and university curriculum.

## Social Control and the Construction of Identity

The disciplines of the sportsfield are not unrelated to wider patterns of social conformity or, for that matter, to the more martial discipline of the parade ground. But it is not only in physical education that the traditional curriculum inculcates social control. The issue of education and social control is amply documented (Grace 1978). What needs to be done here is to identify the latter as a traditionalistic aspect of school and university curricula. As well as being explicit in the religious and social subjects discussed above, the ethos of control saturates the very processes of learning. Take modern foreign languages, in Europe predominantly English. Pupils in Europe are learning English both in state schools and privately from a very early age. Children as young as four in the Netherlands, Greece or Romania will have begun to study English. The mental rigours here might well be compared with the discipline of the sportsfield. Hard, abstract knowledge has to be learned and tested; the multitude of exceptions overcome; the diabolic English orthographic rules and exceptions to be learned; the idiosyncrasies of the ever-changing idiom of English enjoyed or at least tolerated. All this often with very little social contact with native speakers. Given that the academic, social or commercial use of English may be decades away, access to films and pop music cannot conceal the fact that gratification is being very much delayed. What these often very young children are learning is what may be favourably referred to as generic study skill: they are learning to learn, to investigate, to be evaluated. Less favourably expressed, they are learning to be controlled, to postpone their own interests and priorities in exchange for what they are told are their long-term academic and financial interests. The formation of the bilingual identity may be simultaneous with the creation of the frustrated, mercenary personality.

That schools are institutions with high levels of surveillance raises an attractively Foucauldian theme (Foucault 1979; Popkewitz 1997) without tying it sufficiently to the area of curriculum. But this surveillance is actually largely directed to the evaluation of intellectual and social performance and in this it is clearly curriculum-related. Pupils and students are watched to assess their social skills in co-operation, team-building, innovation and competition. But in particular it is their intellectual products – spoken, written, sung, drawn, danced – which are the subject of continuous evaluative scrutiny from the first day in kindergarten through to the PhD examination. The traditional curriculum is much given to testing, examination and assessment. Among the things which pupils and students learn through these oft-repeated activities are that they are the subjects of evaluation; that, no matter how they or their families may wish to value and evaluate them, it is these external mechanisms which will ultimately determine the measure of their true worth. These external measures are then internalized by the subjects and frequently by their families as well. When children subjected to mathematics tests experience repeated failures, they come to construct themselves as not-very-good-at-maths. Subjected thus, and inscribing these failures onto their own identity formation, they will re-asses their reformulated future prospects. Being not-very-good-at-maths has consequences for one's future in the workplace. But a properly restructured identity can mean that one is able to deal with such disappointments as if they were a reasonable part of personal destiny. Educational surveillance and evaluation, as part of a tradition-alist curriculum, assists in the formation of subjected and controlled identities, which are unlikely to question the stratification of either the academy or society.

It is in the task of the legitimation of the state's monopoly of internal and external violence that the school and university curricular systems of Europe face perhaps their most difficult challenge. They are not the only institutions involved in this significant task. Althusser's classic essay spelt out the whole repertoire of what he called repressive and ideological state apparatuses (Althusser 1972). In giving primacy to educational institutions, Althusser might even have overesti-mated their importance. One and a half million Latvians apparently had little difficulty in holding on to the concept of the Latvian nation despite all the Soviet ideological and repressive apparatuses could do to internationalize (Russify) them. But this example is perhaps the wrong way round. The central theme of this chapter is the strength of traditionalistic forces. In this case the language group and the family became the bastion of these forces until such a time as the state could be (re)captured and they could again be constituted inside educational institutions. The speed of transition in this case makes the functions and processes more visible. Yet throughout Europe it is taken for granted that educational insti-tutions should serve to uphold the legitimacy of the state through their curricula. The opposite case would be sociologically unthinkable: that a state should permit and even finance a system that sought to bring about its downfall. History lessons, civics classes, courses in constitutional government, economics and politics all seek to reproduce the norms of the particular state and to present them in a positive and successful light: democracy, capitalism (or, once, communism), constitutional government, the monarchy, the republic, the laity, the church, centralism, federalism, the European Union, isolation from the European Union; all may be identified in the school and university curricula of different European states, each conforming to the accepted political orthodoxy of a particular place and time.

Perhaps Althusser's structuralist hypothesis did not go far enough. What is being inscribed in such courses and lessons, as well as when supporting the national football team or visiting a national historic shrine – so frequently archaeological museums or sites (Diaz-Andreu and Champion 1996) – is the internalization of a national or ethnic identity. Identity construction is the postmodern formulation of what, in this case, Durkheim or Althusser might have seen as social control or social reproduction. It is a no less overarching concept. School and university curricula (along with churches, sporting clubs, newspapers and media, families, language and cultural clubs and communities, heritage tourism) serve to ensure that as each individual is engaged in the process of identity formation or reformation, a central inscription will consist in the taken-for-granted rightness of the principles and practices of the state concerned. The resulting citizenry – collective – thus celebrate rather than question the state's monopoly of the means of warfare.

## Tradition, Culture and Civilization as We Know it

Within the traditionalistic elements in the school and university curriculum, the reproduction of tradition itself has an important place. In Europe – and elsewhere – this is frequently codified inside a particular version of world events which gives the continent a peculiarly unified and central role. Obviously tradition *per se* is a component of the construction of identity within the terms of state legitimation outlined in the previous section. However, in many countries in Europe a notion of the particular history and even destiny of the continent as a whole is embedded in the curriculum. Unitariness is part of this notion. Perhaps derived from the medieval concept of Christendom which preceded Europe as the politically and morally defined cartographic category (Hale 1993), this tradition sees the history and development of the continent as being essentially interconnected. This is well expressed by Delanty:

> Though the idea of Europe rarely evokes the same degree of irrational reverence and deification that the ideal of the national community can demand, it is also ultimately based on an obscurantist interpretation of community: a fantasy homeland that goes hand in hand with a retrospective invention of history as well as a moralisation of geography. Underlying this are unifying narratives of origin and destiny. The difference is that in the case of the idea of Europe it is the mystique of civilisation that is cultivated and reinforced by myths of high culture.
>
> (Delanty 1995: 7–9)

Critically this concerns the impact of various historical periods and developments centred in particular states, cities and epochs of the continent as a whole. The more recent ascendancy of cities such as Amsterdam and London might remain contentious. Much more widely accepted are the influence of fourth-century Athens, classical Rome and Renaissance Italy (including Rome and Venice, but critically Florence). In its crudest, and far from uncommon form, this narrative suggests that European civilization, frequently confused with human civilization in its entirety, originated in Athens, was spread throughout the continent and beyond by republican and imperial Rome and was rescued from the ashes of obscurantism by Renaissance Florence. Europe itself is seen as the cradle of human civilization and culture. The potency of this discursive strategy means that the entire rhetoric and lexicon of culture and civilization must be suspect. The discursive strategy of 'European civilization' or 'European culture' forms the continent-wide parallel to the discourse of heritage used to reproduce nationalism at the level of individual states. On a visit to London in the 1930s Gandhi was asked what he thought of English civilization. He replied that he thought it would be a good idea.

The history curriculum in England and Wales provides an example of the pervasiveness of the traditionalistic stress on Ancient Greece as a founding civilization for Europe. Between the ages of seven and eleven children should study,

> the way of life, beliefs and achievements of the people living in Ancient Greece and the influence of their civilisation on the world today. . . . The city states of Athens and Sparta; gods and goddesses, myths, legends, beliefs and customs; Pheidippides and the battle of Marathon; Pericles and the building of the Parthenon; the conquests of Philip of Macedon and Alexander the Great; great scholars and discoverers.
>
> (Department for Education and Employment 1999: 4)

With a foundation such as this, children and young people in England and Wales will readily be able to grasp the complexities of current Balkan politics.

In curricular terms this traditionalistic discourse of Europe is by no means confined to the subject of history. Indeed the width of its application, proves, for its adherents, an important component of its attractiveness. What is at issue here is a form of Eurocentrism, which tends to see positive developments in all fields of human endeavour originating in Europe and which commensurately sees all developments in Europe as being positive.

- In politics, Athens is the birthplace of democracy and democracy is the one best system, subsequently adopted by all (civilized) countries; Rome is the codifier of law, citizenship and rights.
- In science, medicine and scientific enquiry are both seen to originate in Ancient Greece (Aristotle, Hypocrates); modern science is seen as an exclusively European set of activities and discoveries, with particular states stressing the importance of their protagonists (Bacon, Newton and Darwin against Descartes, Pasteur and Curie); European science is, strangely, seen as an exclusively progressive and beneficial form of intellectual endeavour.
- Philosophy again originated with Socrates and Plato in Athens; non-European belief systems are not categorized as philosophy but as religion, folklore, superstition or other Orientalist appellations; European philosophy is seen as a great tradition, with one mighty mind building on the achievements of his/her (though usually his) predecessors in a movement which has flowed backwards and forwards across the continent from Edinburgh to Koeningsberg.
- In the arts curricula the poetry, drama, oratory, architecture and sculpture of

Athens again take pride of place. The formation of canons in subjects such as literature, music, architecture and art renders the Eurocentric criteria of selection particularly visible in these areas. The fact that one can generalize across such a wide field of human activity is itself an acknowledgement of the rigour with which these canons have been assembled and maintained. In all these curricular areas, though music with its later emergent notation provides an exception in its early professed antecedents, at school and university level in Europe there will typically be stress on the Athenian period, the achievements of Rome, the Renaissance (generally Italian) then (specific to the particular state) the Romantic movement and subsequent nineteenth century classical works (*War and Peace, The Betrothed, The Niebelung's Ring*, the Giverny canvases) before a consideration of the late modern period where local artistic production may be seen as due the most sustained attention.

In knowledge terms, Europe has become its own subject. Both traditional and modern curricular formations betray a solipsistic fascination with the past, not only of individual states or nations but of the continent as a whole. Despite the imperialistic adventures, despite the heterogeneity of the people and cultures resident within Europe, the material taught in schools and universities rarely ventures to explore matters within a genuinely international framework. There are two important dimensions to this limitation: first the achievements and products of non-European societies are neglected; second the impacts of one culture on another and the flow of ideas, people and materials between societies is rarely fully analysed. The concept of a unitary Europe is itself important in the production and reproduction of an ethnocentric, traditionalistic knowledge system.

## Modernity and Postmodernity: Their Impact on Curricular Systems

Having identified at some length traditionalistic elements within European knowledge protocols, this chapter now turns to modernity and postmodernity. The distinction between traditional, modern and postmodern elements in curricular systems (Coulby and Jones 1995) is not intended as a taxonomy. It is not suggested that either a particular state's curriculum or a subject within it could be categorized as belonging to one of these three types. Nor is it intended as a chronology. Modern elements did not replace tradition systematically in a given system; still less are they currently being superseded by potmodernity. Traditional and modern elements remain mixed within the ways in which subjects are defined: even science rests on elements of tradition (notions of madness and sanity); even theology makes some acknowledgment of modernity (acrobatic attempts to reconcile Genesis and Darwin). Postmodernity is scarcely a recognisable element in any European curricular system. However, it provides a strong and wide-ranging critique of traditional and, especially, modernistic knowledge systems. To the extent to which history can be conceptualized as an anti-sexist subject or pupils studying mathematics are aware of Indian and Islamic antecedents, it may be seen to be an emergent component in conflicts over knowledge protocols and curriculum formations. The terms traditional, modern and postmodern, then, provide only a way of describing elements within curricular systems, or, better, components in those ongoing conflicts through which they are determined; they provide a rudimentary lexicon within which the covert politicization of school and university knowledge can be made somewhat more visible.

Modernity as a knowledge system has been associated with the Enlightenment in terms such as the Enlightenment project or the Enlightenment movement. Enlightenment thinkers believed in the power of knowledge, and that societies would inevitably be improved the more widely this power was disseminated. Schools and universities would improve the quality of individual human lives and simultaneously the prosperity and well-being of societies. The effect of the development of late-seventeenth-century science and philosophy was to open up possibilities for the human mind, which became increasingly the measure of all things: it was able to understand and codify with astonishing exactitude and predictability the orderings of the universe and the physical and mental nature of humanity itself.

It is science which lies at the centre of Modernist knowledge: science as a form of classification (Linnaeus), as a record of heroic discoveries and theorization (*The Origin of Species*) and as a method of achieving truth (*Conjectures and Refutations*). More even than this, the Enlightenment saw science as a way of improving the human condition through industrial progress, medicine and public health and, not least, education. However, in retrospect, it can be seen that the effects of modernist knowledge, and of the belief in the universal efficacy of science in particular, have been far from unambiguously beneficial. Enlightenment science perceives nature as something to be explored, classified, experimented with, exploited and dominated. In polluted atmospheres and oceans, in depletion of genetic diversity and in the uneven distribution of medical wellbeing, to pass briefly across important themes, the technological, ecological and human limitations of this approach are increasingly visible.

The social sciences are also a product of modernism. The application of academic, preferably scientific, rigour to individual and social conditions and difficulties effectively begins in the Enlightenment. Adam Smith, Compte, Marx, Durkheim and Binet demonstrate that systematic analysis of social and individual data can apparently reveal both knowledge about the human condition and possible strategies for its amelioration. Modernist social science emphasized the importance of data collection; the application of social and individual data to practical circumstances; the establishment of a canon of revered authorities. Almost as much as through biology and geology, it was through the social sciences that modernism most emphatically distanced itself from religion.

The impact of modernist knowledge on the curriculum of schools and universities has varied between countries. Whilst the French curriculum can be seen in modernist terms at least since the time of Napoleon, in England and Wales a tendency towards a more traditionalist curriculum persisted during the nineteenth century. The stress on religious education, the essentialist concentration on the 'three Rs' and the high status that continued to be awarded to the classics indicate successful resistance to modernism. Technical and scientific education arrived surprisingly late in England and Wales, and vocational technical education has never been established with the success achieved in states such as Germany. Similarly, the continued importance of the churches in schools and higher education, as well as revised governmental emphasis on religious education and daily acts of worship in school, indicate that modernism has not yet completely dominated the English and Welsh curriculum.

There have been at least three major critiques of modernist knowledge: the feminist critique, the culturalist critique and the class critique. It is within these critiques, as well as the more general reassessment of the Enlightenment project, and particularly science, that the impact of postmodernity on curricular systems can most readily be recognized. It is possibly the feminist critique that has had the most radical effect on the supremacy of modernist knowledge. This critique reveals that history, culture, science and technology are, fallaciously, seen to be the exclusive products of men and are so presented within the curricula of schools and universities. Academic history is too often the history of what men did, written by men and taught by men. Literary and cultural studies privilege the work of men and the domains in which men have chosen to work. The activities and achievements of women are hidden, undervalued and denied. The undermining of the male, white, imperialistic narratives of the Enlightenment project is one of the significant achievements of postmodernist theory.

The culturalist critique follows the same pattern as that made by feminism. Modernist knowledge is white, Western knowledge. It is constructed according to what white Western society has seen to be important. It relegates the knowledge of other cultures to superstition or ignorance. It only recognizes academic, scientific and cultural achievement within a very few countries: those of Europe and, belatedly, the United States. The activities and achievements of the rest of humanity are effectively ignored, patronized or belittled within modernist knowledge. This connects modernist knowledge as well as the traditionalism examined above to nationalism and ethnocentricity. Modernist knowledge with its assertion of scientific, political and technological superiority, like traditionalistic knowledge with its confidence of religious rightness, have been used to justify the subjugation and enslavement of whole peoples. Modernist knowledge is incomplete in a number of major ways. First, it finds it difficult to recognize the knowledge, culture and science generated outside Western Europe and its offshoots in North America. Second, it cannot acknowledge the major contributions to Europe's own knowledge and culture made by other traditions. Finally, it hides from its responsibility for the worst excesses of slavery and colonialism.

The third major critique is based on class. Marx commented on the relationship between economic power and cultural and epistemological values:

> The ideas of the ruling class are in every epoch the ruling ideas, i.e. the class which is the ruling material force of society is at the same time its ruling intellectual force. The class which has the means of material production at its disposal, has control at the same time over the means of mental production. . . . The ruling ideas are nothing more than the ideal expression of the dominant material relationships, the dominant material relationships grasped as ideas.
>
> (McLellan 1977: 176)

It is not necessary to subscribe uncritically to base–superstructure theory, nor to stick rigidly to the notion of the pre-eminence of the economic, to acknowledge the power of this critique. The consumerist tastes and fashions of the privileged classes are still too easily reified by academics and teachers as artistic, literary or philosophical value systems. The culture of the poor and often even their languages are either neglected or actively suppressed in such modernist knowledge systems. This simultaneously reduces the variety of the curriculum for everybody and alienates a large section of the school population from what the institution is claiming to offer. The poor are then seen to be educationally failing when they do not accept the intrinsic goodness, truth and beauty of rich people's knowledge.

These three critiques of modernist knowledge, each powerful in its own way and with obvious areas of overlap, are not the only elements in the discrediting of the Enlightenment project. Others have been derived from, for instance, perspectives based on more open acknowledgment of different sexual orientations. Furthermore, the cluster of ideas which involve cultural, historical and scientific relativism have also played a part in undermining modernist knowledge. Whilst this may not be the place to explore the wider literature of postmodernism, it is important to stress the debunking of all grand narratives and the withdrawal of confidence in the rational systematization of knowledge (Harvey 1989; Jameson 1991; Lyotard 1984). Science, judged by its technological and ecological results, is seen as a partial activity wildly out of control rather than as a method of establishing truth.

When these critiques are taken together they have shaken the edifice of modernist knowledge. Postmodernity can be seen as the culmination and the aftermath of these critiques. Postmodernism has gone beyond cultural relativism and the celebration of the exotic to epistemological relativism (Feyerabend 1978a, 1978b). No truth system is seen as being superior. Individual taste and discrimination are encouraged, eclecticism prized and all canons subjected to furious attack. This is not simply an historical process with modernism gradually being superseded by postmodernism. In terms of knowledge and culture the proponents of each are currently engaged in a conflict which, in Europe at least, has taken on both a political and educational aspect (Arnonowitz and Giroux 1991; Coulby and Jones 1995, 1996; Cowen 1996b; Kenaway 1996; Popkewitz 1999; Usher and Edwards 1994; Wexler 1995). Nor are the exponents of traditionalist knowledge absent from this conflict. Indeed, as the next section explores, the final decade has seen some remarkable successes for traditionalism in contrasting areas of knowledge.

## The Creation and Re-Creation of Tradition

When the countries of the former Soviet Union gained independence in 1991, their school and university curricula underwent a rapid transformation. The shift to the national language, adoption of English as a first foreign language and the eradication of Marxist-Leninism have all been discussed above. As well as this, history was re-written to emphasize the distinctiveness of the nation. To take Latvia as a not untypical example, the history of the independent state between 1919 and its illegal suppression by the Soviet Union in 1940 could emerge as an important item of study. Folk music and folk dance that had been, with language, the treasured repository of national identity during the Soviet period, took their important and celebrated part in the school and higher education curriculum. But it was felt that more was needed than this. Scholars looked for ways of rooting the nation, in terms of language and culture, well beyond the brief history of the independent republic. Looking for the kind of cultural legitimation for nationalism and nation building so common in other European countries, they unearthed linguistic histories and in particular sacred texts. Ancient Latvian epics were (re)discovered and brought into the light of curricular day. Lieven describes this process in action:

> Thus the authors of the national epics . . . did indeed 'invent a tradition' which stretched back into an imaginary past and influenced a real national future. This is deliberately symbolised in the episode in *Lacplesis* in which the hero overcomes monsters which guard the scrolls concerning the ancient wisdom of the Latvians in a castle sunk beneath the lake. The epics therefore served three national needs. They were, in the view of the intelligentsia, true 'folk epics', emerging from genuine, ancient folk traditions and 'mirroring

the nation's soul'; they were proof that the Baltic languages could produce great modern writers; and they gave a history, and a sense of history, to peoples who had possessed neither.

(Lieven 1993: 121)

A fractured state in the act of disguising itself as a nation resorts to (or if necessary invents) tradition and then establishes it firmly within the school and university curriculum. Latvia has an ancient literature, therefore Latvia is a nation (and can be made into a state). Latvia's literature is as old and distinguished as that of other European nations (states), therefore Latvia, as a nation and a state is the same as the other European powers. To identify this process in action is not of course to deny either the legitimacy of the Latvian nation or state or the distinction of its literature.

The invention of tradition is commonplace: a classic example is the creation of Scottish costume and ritual by Walter Scot early in the nineteenth century (Hobsbawm and Ranger 1983). It is in neighbouring England and Wales that a parallel example can be found to that of Latvia. Before 1988 the curricula in many schools in the urban areas of England and Wales was veering towards the post-modernist. Anti-racist and anti-sexist initiatives, together with others concerned with generating greater social equality through schooling, had proliferated throughout the then decentralized curricula. This was not to the taste of the then Tory government, whose leader, Thatcher, devoted energy in one of her party conference speeches to deriding anti-racist maths (Bash and Coulby 1989; Coulby and Bash 1991). It was the 1988 Education Act that shifted England and Wales to curricular centralism and which empowered the Secretary of State to draw up and enforce the National Curriculum. This National Curriculum, though subsequently modified (see Department for Education and Employment (1999) for the latest update), is still in place in the state schools of England and Wales. Drawn up by committees firmly under the control of right-wing Secretaries of State, the National Curriculum is an attempt to re-impose a traditionalist curriculum on England and Wales. Subjects such as sociology, politics, media studies and economics, which had been popular up to 1988 in secondary schools, were not included in the National Curriculum, and so disappeared to the margins. Even home economics was considered politically suspect and was incorporated into technology. At primary level, topic-based approaches, still today widespread in countries such as Italy, were condemned and a subject-based, grammar-school curriculum was imposed. The knock on effect of these changes at university level took longer to materialize, but they may well explain the current diminishing popularity of the social sciences in UK higher education.

Anti-racism and anti-sexism were swept with one stroke into the dustbin of curricular history. In their place the Act insisted on Christian religious education and a daily collective act of worship. History is predominantly about the United

Kingdom, with very little coverage of the embarrassing issues such as the colonization of Ireland, the slave trade or the depopulation of the Highlands. English is constrained to grammatical versatility and the study, at all ages, of government approved (and predominantly white, English origin) texts, with Shakespeare leading the traditionalist charge. Music and art are redolent with the products and activities of an exhausted canon. Science, mathematics and technology are constructed within a non-problematic framework that loudly fails to acknowledge the contribution of non-European cultures. This curriculum is accompanied by an equally traditionalistic paraphernalia of regular testing of children and inspecting of schools and teachers. In the hands of new Labour it is leading to extraordinarily high degrees of control over teachers in matters of timetabling and pedagogy as well as curriculum content, initially in the areas of literacy and mathematics.

Traditionalism, modernity and postmodernity are political forces in conflict in all curricular systems in Europe. The extent to which traditionalism and modernism are successful in these conflicts will impact on the recognition given in school and universities to the knowledges and cultures of the many populations of the diverse European society. It may also impact on the ability of states and the business institutions within them to operate successfully in the new international economy. These matters are taken up in the next chapter.

## Discussion Questions

1   Why has religion maintained so much influence on so many aspects of education at different levels?
2   What is the relationship between the assessment of school knowledge and social control?
3   To what extent are school and university curricular systems in the USA Eurocentric?
4   What might a postmodern school or university curriculum look like?

## Further Reading

Marx' essay *On the German Ideology* is a powerful and highly influential statement on the relationship between control of wealth on the one hand and control of knowledge and culture on the other. Its ideas are brought into the framework of political power in Althusser's essay on ideology: Althusser, L. (1972) 'Ideology and the Ideological State Apparatus', in B. R. Cosin (ed.), *Education: Structure and Society*. Harmondsworth, Penguin. Although this is now regarded as an over-determined view, it remains a vigorous attack on the role of school and university knowledge. For this reason it can be a depressing piece for teachers and students to read. Nevertheless, it is necessary to be able to counter some of Althusser's arguments if the profession of teaching is to be seen as being more than the reproduction of government ideology.

It has always surprised me that teachers and those in teacher education find cultural relativism such a frightening position to adopt. Any position of cultural superiority is surely out of place in pluralist societies and classrooms. Feyerabend's position of epistemological relativism, and indeed epistemological anarchy, might be rather more difficult to countenance.

Feyerabend, P. (1978a) *Against Method*. London: Verso.

Feyerabend, P. (1978b) *Science in a Free Society*. London: Verso.

These two books deal with matters of profound epistemological (and therefore curricular) importance but in an accessible and often humorous way.

# 5   The Knowledge Economy

## New Skills in the Workplace

A change is taking place in the global economy. It is simultaneously becoming more internationalized and more centred on knowledge. This change has been boldly theorized by Castells:

> at the end of the twentieth century, we are living through one of these rare intervals in history. An interval characterised by the transformation of our 'material culture' by the works of a new technological paradigm organised around information technologies.
>
> (Castells 1996: 29)

As always when there are changes in the economy, there will be resulting changes in society and not least in education. But the current tranche of rapid and wide-ranging changes actually involves knowledge, the subject of education itself. To this extent schools and university curricula ought to be at the forefront of the implementation of these developments. This chapter examines, among other things, the extent to which this is actually the case.

Given that these developments in both the economy and in education are frequently being led by the United States, as well as the fact that much of the literature is derived from there, this chapter will necessarily make substantial reference to the USA as well as Europe. First it is necessary to provide some overview of the changes which are taking place at the level of investment, production, distribution and consumption, and the new skills necessary to the implementation of these changes. The chapter then considers knowledge itself as an item of world trade. It then looks at universities and schools separately since their response to the emergence of the knowledge economy appears to be markedly different.

Following Reich (in Neef 1998), it is possible to identify three sets of related skills which drive forward high-value businesses. 'First are the problem-solving skills required to put things together in unique ways (be they alloys, molecules, semiconductor chips, software codes, movie scripts, pension portfolios, or

60

information)' (Neef 1998: 49). These skills involve the ability to place components of knowledge together in a meaningful and profitable way. They are not the old-style skills of one-off design where a brilliant prototype can proceed to production. They involve the on-going modification and improvement of the product and its development to whole new sets of applications; consider the progress from MS DOS to Windows NT.

The second set of skills are those required 'to help customers understand their needs and how those needs can best be met by customised products' (Neef 1998: 49). This is not merely a matter of sales and marketing: it requires a genuine and detailed knowledge of the customer's business and how it can be improved. The skills concern the identification of opportunities and the implementation of innovation. Universities, for instance choose a software package to control student choices in a modular scheme, but are then shown how adaptations to the same software can help them track the payment of student fees and the control of library stock.

The third of these sets concerns problem identification and solution conventionally associated with entrepreneurialism. 'People in such roles must understand enough about specific technologies and markets to see the potential for new products,' raise the necessary capital and 'assemble the right problem-solvers and -identifiers to carry it out' (Neef 1998: 49). Rather than being financiers or conventional managers, people with such skills are managers of ideas. These are the skills needed to develop, finance and launch the English Premiere League, say, or a new digital broadcasting corporation or the Eurofighter.

The emerging economy that is based on these skills is effectively one where services have replaced goods. Actual manufacture, even of complex machines, is of decreasing importance. 'In 1984, 80 percent of the cost of a computer was in its hardware, 20 percent in software; by 1990, the proportions were just the reverse' (Neef 1998: 48). High-profit enterprises in the emerging knowledge economy are thus involved in services: 'the specialised research, engineering, and design services necessary to solve problems; the specialised sales, marketing, and consulting services necessary to identify problems; and the specialised strategic, financial, and management services of brokering the first two' (ibid.: 50). Within such an economy managers are no longer responsible principally for people but for the gathering, organization and evaluation of knowledge.

The knowledge needed to sustain and develop such enterprises and to train and update such managers is, in two important ways, international. First, it is being generated and reproduced in a multitude of centres around the world, in Korea, the United States and Japan as well as in the European Union (Castells 1989, 1996, 1997, 1998). The centres where it is developed and reproduced (universities certainly, but also the research and development branches of trans-national corporations and of state governments) are themselves increasingly cosmopolitan in terms of their staffing, their students and researchers and their curricula and knowledge and research projects. Second, knowledge, like finance, people and goods and services is involved in international flows (Lash and Urry 1994). Whether Thurow (in Neef 1998) is right to assume that knowledge moves more slowly than everything else because education 'and training take a long time to complete, and many of the relevant skills are not those taught in formal education institutions but the process skills that can only be learned in a production environment' (Neef 1998: 206), is less clear than the magnitude of the implications of this dimension of economic change for those educational institutions as they struggle to develop in this international context.

This chapter argues that the production, evaluation and exchange of knowledge are increasingly important economic activities; that, indeed, knowledge has become the world's most important and valuable trading commodity. It considers, centrally, the importance of information and communications technology (ICT) within the workplace and the extensive changes that it is brining about. It then goes on to consider the extent to which schools and universities in Europe and the USA have adapted to this important transition.

## Knowledge as a Trading Commodity

Both the product of economic activity and the way in which it is being conducted are changing rapidly. What seems to be occurring is an evolution towards a quartenary economy (here referred to as the knowledge economy), one based on services rather than manufacture. The introduction of ICT into so many processes of financing, design, management, production, distribution and consumption has been a significant stage in this evolution. In response to this the countries of the west and of the Pacific Rim are attempting, with varying degrees of determination, to transform themselves into smart states. In the European states now emerging from command economies, the vital areas of economic knowledge may still be those pertaining to the administration of a capitalist economy and a free market (see the articles in Pinder 1998). Increasingly these skill and techniques are themselves linked to those contained within the wider dimensions of the knowledge economy. This aspiration towards the smart state (Blunkett 1999) obviously has profound implications for the curricula of schools and universities. This section examines the extent to which schools and universities are coming to terms with the extent of the transformative impact of ICT.

At one level it is obvious enough to assert that knowledge is an important trading commodity. Nor is this a new phenomenon. Knowledge of silk weaving or of rubber tapping has moved across the world, making and marring fortunes in the process. From the beginning of the industrial revolution, if not earlier, the knowledge of the skilled mechanic has had its global market as the world-wide spread of Scottish engineers well testifies. But this process has now both widened and deepened. It now applies to an exceedingly wide range of types of expertise, from nuclear physics to the staging of grand opera. The number of skills and areas of expertise within even one activity, be it banking, marketing or genetic engineering, has also expanded dramatically.

Knowledge has emerged as a major trading commodity in the international market. Knowledge and knowledge-based processes both underpin material production and are themselves becoming ever more important aspects of production and consumption. Knowledge of armaments developments, pharmaceutical production and medical techniques are highly sought after across the world. Design, and subsequently marketing, of clothing, cars or food can be more remunerative than their manufacture or sale. The add-on value of 'aestheticisation' (Lash and Urry 1994), often located in western centres such as London, Paris or Milan, generates greater profits than the actual mass manufacture of the commodities concerned, which often takes place in distant locations. The media and publications industries now look to global, multi-media production with a string of associated, franchised products. The design of computer systems, and especially software and operating and filing systems, has facilitated the mushrooming of global monopolies. The economies of the EU and the United States are gradually shifting to this knowledge production and reproduction. Important institutions in this knowledge economy are:

- television, music and film studios, increasingly operating on a small-scale, franchized basis
- publishing houses, including the production of the proliferating, specialist magazines on themes such as sport, computing, leisure
- research and development facilities, especially in ICT, genetic engineering and systems design
- fashion houses and associated designer labels with large-scale marketing industries which can attach them to a whole bundle of products and activities
- specialist journal and conference networks, including those associated with higher education
- and, not least, schools, colleges, universities and research institutes.

Of course all of these themselves have consumption implications, from local area networks to exotic restaurants, which further the shift towards the quaternary economy (Zukin 1988, 1991, 1995).

The movement of pupils and students about the world means that schools and, much more significantly, universities, are themselves traders in knowledge as a commodity. There is stiff competition between universities in the USA, the UK and increasingly Australia to attract students from other states. These universities, either directly or through agencies, have significant marketing facilities in states as various as Malaysia, India and Greece. The English language as much as the standards of the universities in these states mean that they are attractive to students from a wide range of states. It is the high fees the institutions and states can charge, at least as much as any policy towards internationalization, that makes overseas students so attractive. At undergraduate level as well as in the form of PhDs, universities are selling knowledge on a world market. The Secretary of State for Education and Employment in the UK cited 'the education and training industry' as 'earning' seven billion pounds per year in 'exports' (Blunkett 1999).

There are at least two distinct aspects to this emergence of the knowledge economy which are important to states and their educational institutions. First, there is the amount of knowledge which a particular state can generate via its business institutions, research centres and universities; the relevance of this knowledge to the processes of production, distribution and consumption; the extent to which this knowledge is marketable and renewable. While the relevant areas of knowledge in the past have included finance, industrial production, technology and medicine, in the present and the future they are increasingly concerning the development and application of ICT. Second, there is the amount of knowledge which the workforce of a given society can mobilize in economic activity; the extent to which any state has succeeded in becoming a smart society.

In the first category the United States is obviously a state which has been successful in generating large amounts of productive knowledge. It is more difficult to point to a successful example in the second category, though Singapore seems to have done better than the USA or the European states in educating a large proportion of its population to a high degree of productivity within the knowledge economy.

## Educational Institutions in the Knowledge Economy: Universities

In the United States and Western Europe, the shift to a quaternary economy has been accompanied by anxiety about the curriculum, especially that of schools and vocational training institutions. The form of this anxiety has almost universally been a perception of a dissonance between the nature of the school and/or vocational curriculum and the needs of the workplace in terms of particular knowledge, skills and demeanour. Manifestations of this anxiety have included:

- attempts by states to centralize curricula
- an emphasis on (often narrowly defined) vocational skills
- a stress on basic skills, which can be accompanied as in the UK and the USA , by the descant of a restatement of basic values ('back to basics')
- a new emphasis on social skills, the techniques of deference and demeanour.

The response to economic and technological transition, and to an awareness of intensified international competition, has been an attempt to make the curricula of schools and vocational institutions more relevant to those skills and practices apparently needed in the workplace (Bash and Green 1995).

At one level of the workforce, this might have served to supply appropriately trained and quiescent workers to a productive sector which had been substantially deskilled. At the higher and expanding level of the economy, however, this trend can be seen as largely counterproductive in that it fails to recognize the emerging processes and practices of the knowledge economy. The skills needed for this knowledge economy may be strictly vocational, in computer assisted design, in music technology, in ICT itself, but where this is the case, it is higher education, rather than schools and vocational institutions, which is supplying the specialized personnel. In more generic terms the skills of the quaternary economy concern:

- the ability to research a project quickly and effectively using a variety of resources
- a sense of enrepreneurship recodified to include opportunistic behaviour, a commitment to the individual career and the capacity to take risks with other people's money
- the determination to seek out new opportunities for development, often at an international level
- the ability to make attractive and convincing presentations in a variety of media
- the skill to move effortlessly across a range of software applications and network facilities
- the ability to work cooperatively with other people, often from different backgrounds and disciplines
- the ability to operate in English for purposes of both production and consumption
- the determination to make and maintain a large network of important contacts across a range of institutions and activities and with a national or international spread
- the ability to take on a persona which is both corporate collectivist and individually distinctive in terms of cultural consumption.

Again these are more readily identifiable as the skills taught by higher education institutions where arts, humanities and social sciences courses continue to proliferate, and where ICT is rapidly penetrating all areas of work. The expansion of higher education institutions has accompanied and to a certain degree facilitated the expansion in employment prospects for people with this range of skills.

Universities are indeed an essential component of the knowledge economy. Interestingly, this is by no means an exclusively science-centred phenomenon: indeed in the UK several universities have recently closed down their science departments because so few students wish to take these courses at undergraduate level. Certainly technology and ICT departments are generating many of the skills of the knowledge economy, but this is also the case in the never-more-popular arts and humanities courses and in the social sciences. The modularization of higher education and the implementation of government imperatives, via the various quality maintenance arrangements (Cowen 1996a), has assisted in this process. Thus courses on graphic design are as likely to include modules on marketing as on the Renaissance; sociology degrees will include modules investigating strategies used by the mass media or by advertising as well as introducing students to the works of Durkheim and Weber.

Furthermore, universities are themselves one of the major sites of the knowledge economy. Knowledge protocols of many university departments, characterized by the development and expansion of knowledge itself, and the procedures of hypothesis and experimentation, are actually conducive to the activities of the knowledge economy. It is in university research departments that many developments and innovations in science and technology are first made: ICT and genetic engineering being obvious current examples. 'The two sources of the Net, the military/science establishment and the personal computing counterculture, did have a common ground: the university world' (Castells 1996: 355). This is not to imply that these processes are exclusively benign: this would appear to be as far from the case with regard to the commercial applications of genetic technology as it was in earlier phases with regard to armament and pharmaceutical development. University departments have a great impact on design and style in matters as diverse as architecture, fashion and theatrical direction. University publishing houses and specialist journals play an important part in disseminating the recent productions of the knowledge economy. Universities are important users of the worldwide web for both the construction and dissemination of research. Finally, universities are themselves major employers within the knowledge economy. The simultaneous expansion of both higher education and the knowledge economy has led to a significant increase in the number of people employed as academics and researchers.

## Education and the Knowledge Economy: Schools

As producers and reproducers of knowledge, it is the universities rather than the schools, which have responded most readily and substantially to the needs of the quartenary economy. As mentioned at the start of the previous section, politicians and commentators, including those concerned with the knowledge economy itself, have centred their anxieties on schools, particularly in the USA and the UK. Neef writes 'Unfortunately, in the US and Britain, particularly, there are indications that the education and training infrastructure necessary to provide these knowledge based skills broadly throughout the population is becoming both inadequate and inappropriate for the knowledge-based economy' (Neef 1998: 9). He and others link this to the likelihood of unemployment and marginalization for a significant section of the population, while, by contrast, those educated in the skills of the knowledge economy continue to thrive.

Rosecrance (in Neef 1998) draws attention to the lack of investment in schooling in some states, in particular to the low salaries paid to teachers. He contrasts that with the salaries paid in Switzerland (about twice that in the UK, France or the USA), with the implication that higher salaries will attract better skilled teachers and thus help develop superior schools. In terms of vocational education and apprenticeship there is again a dissonance between the skills offered and those needed (see the bullet-point list in the previous section) in the knowledge economy. The exception here is Germany, where the vocational education system is almost universally admired. Smith, for instance, (in Neef 1998) cites Thurow as seeing the education of those who do not go to university as being 'the German secret weapon' (Neef 1998: 231). He believes that

> after you get through a German apprenticeship training program, you're simply the best educated person in the world at your level. They turn out an absolutely world-class worker, and it allows them to make very sophisticated products, use very sophisticated machine tools, and operate technologies at levels that the rest of the world finds impossible to operate.
>
> (Neef 1998: 231)

Smith and other commentators, perhaps too readily, link this strength in training to the success of the German economy. The story is of course more complicated, referring to patterns of investment, post-war renewal and the fact that Germany's economy remains much more concentrated on manufacture than those of the UK, France or the Netherlands (Marsden and Marsden 1995). Nevertheless, the importance of the commitment of German industry and commerce to the maintenance of the high-quality apprenticeship scheme is almost universally admired and envied.

The failure of schools to address the needs of the knowledge economy may come to be matched by a shift of education, as opposed to childcare, to the private sector. Davis and Botkin (in Neef 1998) believe that corporations rather than states are making the changes in education necessary for the knowledge economy. They lament the fact that school systems

> are lagging behind the transformation that is evolving outside them, in the private sector at both work and play, with people of all ages. Over the next few decades, the private sector will eclipse the public sector as our predominant educational institution.
>
> (Neef 1998: 164)

While the strengths identified in universities in the previous section will probably tend to falsify this bold hypothesis, it certainly highlights the extent of the weaknesses perceived in the school system. Panaceas for educational change are rarely difficult to find and this chapter will struggle to eschew such utopianism. A particularly noteworthy example (Colardyn and Durand-Drouhin in Neef 1998), however, demonstrates ways in which schools might replicate the processes as well as the topics of the knowledge economy, for example 'just-in-time learning'.

> This means acquiring skill or knowledge at the time or place where it is needed, instead of learning it ahead of time and in a different place. . . . Like just-in-time inventory control, just-in-time learning avoids unnecessary investment and minimizes deterioration of knowledge and skill from non-use. The need to solve an immediate problem also provides both a motivation to learn and a context that makes new information meaningful.
>
> (Neef 1998: 250)

If there is a lack of contact between schools (though not universities so much) and the needs of the knowledge economy then there are at least two sets of reasons. The first concerns the tendency towards centralizing the curriculum discussed in the second chapter of this book. The second concerns the education, status and remuneration of the teaching force. In both these sets of reasons, which are discussed in the remainder of this chapter, ICT is a main element. Before addressing these arguments, however, it is necessary to eschew any facile, economistic link between schools and society. A transformation of school curricula will not in itself bring about economic restructuring. This is well stated by Carnoy and Fluitman:

> Despite the apparent consensus around the supply-side, skill mismatch argument, the supporting evidence for it is extremely thin, especially in terms of improved education and more and better training solving either the problem of open unemployment (Europe) or the problem of wage distribution (US). It is much more convincing, we argue, that better education and more training could, in the longer run, contribute to higher productivity and economic growth rates.
>
> (quoted in Castells 1996: 274)

The school and university curricula do not directly control the size or the nature of the workforce. They may, however, have a long-term effect on the nature of economic activity, the place that workers play within it and the level of their employability and remuneration.

There is a lack of articulation then, to return to the main argument, between the centralizing curricula of school systems and the needs of the emerging knowledge economy. The state control of school knowledge appears not to be bringing it into closer harmony with the current and future needs of the workplace. The knowledge protocols espoused by those taking control of the school curriculum are more relevant to previous phases of European development than to current and future needs. Across Europe national politicians are very keen to attract foreign direct investment, especially in high-tech industries and services, yet, as they take increasing control over the content of the school curriculum, they appear to be neglecting the very skills necessary for such economic success. Why? It could be that these politicians and their advisers are unaware of international economic trends and the way they are likely to impact on schools. But this seems far-fetched. This chapter offers three sets of reasons: those concerned with a distracted agenda; those concerning the necessary expenditure; and those concerning the nature and skills of the teaching force.

The distracted agenda concerns the priorities that politicians set themselves. In the UK, Greece and the Netherlands as well as in the United States, these have recently been concerned with 'standards'. Often drawing on international comparators of dubious value and the cargo-cult discourse of comparative education (Cowen 1998), politicians have described national school standards of achievement either as falling or as not improving as rapidly as those of major economic competitors. Indeed one of the major legitimations for the introduction of the National Curriculum in England and Wales, as for other educational policy initiatives in Europe, was professed concern about standards. Thus politicians took control of what was taught in schools, while paradoxically their real (at least expressed) concern was with the level of children's attainment within these subjects. Furthermore, a professed concern with standards could only focus on those areas which the public considered to be important (state language and mathematics) and where, to give the whole intervention a spurious veneer of objectivity, national and international comparative data appeared to be available (mathematics and science, but also state languages, and, outside the UK and Ireland, English). In this exercise in supposedly raising standards, the relation between the content of the curriculum and changes in the global economy fell from sight. The National Curriculum in England and Wales was taken for granted, in fact in its conception it bore an anachronistic similarity with the pre-war grammar school curriculum (Aldrich 1988). The distraction of the beguiling standards initiatives meant that politicians lost sight not of what was being taught but rather of the need to ensure some congruence between what was being taught and the changes that their *Financial Times* would every day have shown them to be taking place in the economy.

The other distraction was that politicians were much more confident about what ought *not* to be taught in schools. Previous chapters have shown how in England and Wales knowledge areas considered to be in any way progressive, such as sociology or economics, and approaches to the curriculum associated with interculturalism or anti-sexism were systematically excluded from the National Curriculum. More generally, the point has been made that centralized national curricular systems tend to generate nationalist curricula. The political discourse on standards combined with the impulsion towards traditional, nationalist values and culture in the 'back-to-basics' movement of the early 1990s in the UK and the USA. This explicitly reactionary agenda appeared to be taking place in an economic vacuum. The school curriculum, but not that of universities, was being shifted back apparently to prepare children and young people for the workplace of the industrial revolution.

A second set of reasons for the disarticulation between school curricula and the knowledge economy concerns the mind-boggling expense of introducing ICT into classrooms. Across Europe and the United States politicians developed a fear of increasing state expenditure on education (a possible exception is Switzerland, though not high state-spending Denmark, which long maintained a technophobic stance with regard to the impact of computers in schools). This derived from the belief that any government which increased direct taxation would never be re-elected. Unfortunately for this view, in order for schools to participate in and prepare pupils for the network society, they would need to have the kind of provision now emerging in European universities:

- local area networks with web access
- specialist teaching rooms with computers, printers, software and peripherals available for every student
- generic classrooms with several computers and with facility for computer projection and presentation
- all staff skilled in generic ICT skills
- staff skilled in the applications of ICT to their particular subject.

The costs here are fearsome despite the falling prices for ICT hardware which have characterized the last two decades. The electrical, cabling, security, safety and software costs exceed those of the hardware. In addition there would be the need to skill-up an entire generation of teachers. Not only that, but as the technology is changing so rapidly (at the level of the chip itself from the 386 to the pentium 3 in one decade), politicians could be just about sure that any investment they made would not be future-proof but would need to be renewed every three years. Faced with these difficulties, the temptation to bury the policy-making head in the distractions of the standards debate became all the more beguiling. The rich suburbs of American cities have long been an exception to this generalization and others are beginning to emerge. The latest, draconian, centralized initiative on teacher education in England and Wales stipulates the precise ICT competencies needed by both primary and secondary teachers alike, in both generic skills and those related to their particular subject. The effectiveness of this initiative remains to be evaluated.

It is the nature of the teaching profession, its remuneration and access to relevant training which forms the final set of reasons for the reluctance of schools in Europe and the USA to come to terms with the knowledge economy. In many states of Europe, such as Germany, the Netherlands and the UK, there is a different preparation for primary teachers than for secondary. In general terms the former are educated in new universities or *hogeschools* whilst the latter are educated in old universities. Within Europe there are great differences in the duration and rigour of teacher education. In France, where primary and secondary arrangements are parallel, students must first have a degree, which is likely to take four years to obtain; then they must attend an IUFM to take either the CAPES or CAPEP. In either case, the Certificate takes two years to complete and the failure rate between year one and two can be as high as 50 per cent. In the UK a primary teacher can be prepared by a three-year BEd course, and a secondary teacher can go straight into school after the first, three year degree, and qualify as a teacher while actually working in school. Not surprisingly the status of the teaching force and their perceived job satisfaction, though interestingly not their remuneration, is higher in France than in the UK. With regard to remuneration, with the exception of Switzerland (Rafferty 1998) and some rich suburbs of the United States (Knapp and Woolverton 1995), teachers' salaries have been perceived to be falling relative to those of other professional workers for the last two decades.

The concern with standards has led in many states to a concentration on the training, evaluation, control and regimentation of the teaching force. This concentration on surveillance, discipline and control has been well characterized by Foucault (Foucault 1979). These policies include:

- strict state control over the institutions and curricula of initial teacher education (sometimes revealingly referred to as training)
- a similar state involvement in in-service education, often focused on the perceived immediate needs of the classroom at the expense of, say, Masters-level study
- regular and arduous inspections of schools by state agencies, often with publicly available reports, sometimes resulting in political and journalistic criticism or indeed pillorying
- national testing in curriculum subjects deemed to be core, sometimes leading to the compilation of national or regional league tables on the basis of results
- national curriculum systems
- a lack of trust in the professionalism of teachers and headteachers, manifested through the involvement of politicians and businesspeople in the governance of schools
- the introduction of appraisal arrangements, sometimes linked to levels of remuneration
- an attempt to devise mechanisms for sacking teachers perceived to be ineffective
- pay rises either below inflation or phased, or both

71

- attempts to link teachers' salaries to their performance during inspections or to their pupils' performance in national tests
- a climate of criticism amounting sometimes to undisguised hostility in the statements of politicians and journalists of both left- and right-wing persuasions.

Obviously England and Wales provides the case example here, where all the above elements can be found. Many can also be readily identified, however, in states as varied as France, the Netherlands and Romania. They characterize some elements of the reform programme introduced in 1998 (Law 2525/1997), to widespread student hostility in Greece (Zambeta 1999).

There are at least two consequences of these policies for the capacity of states to bring their school curricula closer to the needs of the knowledge economy. First, in the UK, the Netherlands and Russia, though not in France or Greece, teaching is ceasing to be an attractive profession. Especially when the European economy is booming, pupils with high-school leaving qualifications or students with good degrees will be attracted into better paid, less regulated and less stigmatized professions. In the long term this will result in a less qualified teaching force, lower morale and teacher shortages. Graduates and school leavers with high level ICT and system skills are precisely the ones who will most readily obtain employment in the knowledge economy and not be attracted to working in schools. Even draconian state interventions in teacher education may be insufficient to remedy the ICT skills shortage among teachers if they take place against the background of the other policies just mentioned, which deter entry into the profession. Second, these policies result in an existing teaching force, demoralized by stigmatization and poor pay, overburdened with bureaucratic work requirements of regular inspections and national assessment schemes, and bemused and fatigued by successive waves of government education reform. There is a danger that such a teaching force has lost the professional freedom and capacity to behave pro-actively in curriculum matters. The consequence of state policies with regard to the profession itself means that governments cannot look to teachers to rescue them from the shortsightedness of their centralized school curriculum initiatives.

## Discussion Questions

1 Sociologists are ever prone to announce fundamental changes in society. How significant do you consider the development of the knowledge economy to be?
2 Is the chapter correct in identifying a differential response, as between schools and universities, to the knowledge economy?
3 Which states, regions and groups are likely to benefit from the knowledge economy and which lose?
4 Are teachers in schools agents or victims of distracted curricular agenda?

## Further Reading

When I was researching this book I could not find Neef's collection in either the Education or the Sociology section of Dillons. I had to go the Management section. At that point it seemed as if I were following a rather esoteric interest. Now the phrase 'knowledge economy' is already a political and journalistic commonplace.

D. Neef's edited volume, (1998) *The Knowledge Economy*, Boston: Butterworth-Heineman, is a challenge for those in universities and especially schools. The fact that academics and practitioners in management were involved in this area before those in education indicates the distance the latter may need to travel.

Castells has always held a negative and slighting view of schools. His three volumes on the Information Age maintain this tradition. They do however provide a wide ranging overview of changes in the global economy and the ways in which these are and are not being generated by developments in knowledge, especially in ICT.

Castells, M. (1996) *The Information Age: Economy, Society and Culture*. Oxford: Blackwell.

Castells, M. (1997) *The Information Age: Economy, Society and Culture*. Oxford: Blackwell.

Castells, M. (1998) *The Information Age: Economy, Society and Culture*. Oxford: Blackwell.

# 6 Modernist Knowledge and Prejudice: Special Educational Needs

## Introduction

This chapter examines the curricular and assessment systems of schools and universities in Europe with regard to their function in legitimating and embodying particular views of special educational need. (The concept of need in this categorization is not taken for granted but opened to question in the course of the chapter.) Other authors have examined the ways in which the processes and indeed the structures of schooling serve to pick out some children and young adults as being, in whatever way, different (Garner and Sandow 1995; Sandow 1995). These differences then become the focus for educational interventions in the learning, the life style and indeed the life chances of the individuals concerned. What differentiates this individual from others, rather than what s/he may have in common with them, then becomes the focus for intense educational – or medical, psychological, psychiatric or whatever – interest and activity. Much remains to be done to rectify these processes and structures. It is the contention of this chapter, however, that these processes and structures themselves are underpinned by knowledge systems and knowledge protocols which, in so far as they impact on children and young people perceived to have special educational needs, have remained largely unchallenged. This chapter examines first knowledge systems, and then knowledge protocols.

## Knowledge Systems: Science and Normality

As mentioned in Chapter Four and explored further in Chapter Eight, knowledge systems have been subjected to a critique from a position which might be broadly categorized as postmodernist. Modernist knowledge has been seen as being sexist: it is knowledge about men, men's activities, achievements and interests, constructed by men, according to criteria and values which are important to men. The roles of women in knowledge and the criteria they might apply to its construction and organization have largely been ignored. Similarly, as far back as Marx, knowledge and culture had been seen to be those skills, products and activities most pleasing to the ruling class of any particular epoch and most likely to assist in the extension of their wealth and power. In Chapter Four traditionalist and modernist knowledge systems were characterized as Eurocentric, white and racist.

Parallel critiques have been made from a variety of particular positions: to take two more examples, gay rights and environmentalism. Knowledge has been seen to privilege heterosexual forms of human relationships. The achievement of homosexual people in cultural, scientific, political and other areas has been concealed, disguised, marginalized or sanitized. Homophobic prejudice has been reinforced by school and university knowledge. The way in which the Aids scare has been transposed into health education is an example of this. Health education plays into the media presentation of HIV as a disease of *others*: Africans, drug users, homosexuals. Environmentalists and ecofeminists have found modernist versions of knowledge inadequate to meet the crises of unequal distribution and pollutive and unsustainable production. The knowledge of schools and universities is almost exclusively that which will perpetuate modes of production and consumption that exacerbate the ecological crises. Modernist knowledge as transmitted in European schools and universities does not offer forms of production and behaviour that might serve to avert or even diminish these crises (Hicks and Slaughter 1998).

A parallel critique of modernist knowledge with regard to people who are perceived in various ways to be disabled is still emerging (Daniels and Garner 1999). It is of particular importance to the institutions of education, since these are the sites where knowledge is legitimated and reproduced for those perceived to be disabled. Equally, but not so obviously important, they are the sites where knowledge is legitimated and reproduced for those not so perceived, indeed for those making the perception. In this respect, this chapter focuses on science and in particular medicine. However, it is a mode of analysis that needs to be conducted with regard to a whole range of curricular areas. How much of the literature studied in schools and universities, for instance, has been written by people perceived to be disabled? To what extent does the educational canon of literature accurately reflect the experiences of such people, distort these experiences or ignore them altogether (*Jane Eyre, Jude the Obscure, The Idiot*)? Parallel, though less easily formulated, questions can be asked of music and art (*Lucia di L'ammermoor, Boris Godunov, The Scream*). The romanticization and marginalization of madness is not without influence on the process of identity formation. To what extent does school and university history address the circumstances of people perceived to be disabled and their relationships with each other and with people not so perceived; what provisions and institutions were created for them; what philosophies underpinned and legitimated these forms and processes? In this case, of course, Foucault (1967, 1973) has provided some of the answers. However, the Foucauldian view of *Madness and Civilization* and *The Birth of the Clinic* is not one that has progressed very far in the European school and university history curriculum.

In all subjects the questions of representation, and especially inclusion, remain. To what extent do examples and illustrations in science and technology texts emphasize the activities, achievements and potentialities of those perceived to be disabled? Stephen Hawkins has recently become, at least in the UK, a widely-known example of such achievement. To what extent does the discourse of educational subject knowledge across the school and university curriculum stress the arrangements, facilities and technologies necessary to facilitate total inclusion? It is the argument of this chapter that it is school and university knowledge as a whole, but particularly the university study of medicine and educational psychology, which produce and legitimate special educational need as well as the wider patterns of stratification examined in preceding chapters.

Science, especially the university level subjects of medicine and educational psychology, is the central subject with regard to the way in which school and university knowledge excludes and stigmatizes those perceived to be disabled. Medical students at London University are privileged to be able to visit a collection of 'freaks' (scare quotes proliferate in this area). The skeleton of 'the Elephant Man', for instance, has not been respectfully laid to rest but is there for the critical attention of such students. The exhibiting of such people did not end even after death. What is here in an extreme form is a set of confusions that underpin western medicine. Health is associated inextricably with normality. Health and normality are associated with well-being and even with benevolence. It is the opposite formulation of these confusions which affect people perceived to be 'disabled': difference from the artificially constructed norm is equated with sickness, with misfortune and, even more tendentiously, with malevolence. In the reverse process, that which is criminal or wicked is seen as being necessarily unhealthy or unbalanced (Szasz 1972); consider the use of words such as 'twisted', 'psycho' or 'sick'. It is science here that makes the association which literature and popular culture can readily take up and amplify in the strand which ties the unusual to the malevolent via sickness (the psychopath, for instance, in crime fiction or Hollywood movies, the association of 'deformity' with evil from *Richard III* to *Don't Look Now*).

The medicine which is taught at universities in Europe, and the school science which feeds into it, is a knowledge system which supports the segregation and stigmatization of those perceived to be different, both in educational institutions and – far from unconnectedly – in wider society. As Illich asserted:

> With the development of the therapeutic service sector of the economy, an increasing proportion of all people come to be perceived as deviating from some desirable norm, and therefore as clients who can now either be submitted to therapy to bring them closer to the established standard of

health or concentrated into some special environment built to cater to their deviance.

(Illich 1976)

School and university science does this because it is committed to a notion of normality that is restricted in terms of physical and behavioural and even cosmetic conformity. Its attitude and response to that which fails to conform to its normality may be prurient, excluding, invasive, stigmatizing and often punitive.

To substantiate this rather sweeping statement the argument goes on to consider four of the main tools of western medicine: pharmaceuticals, invasive surgery, 'counselling' and pre-natal screening.

Pharmaceuticals are increasingly being used to control people's behaviour and even emotions. Pills and medication help people to sleep, to behave in a socially acceptable way, to feel good about themselves and to be happy. Some, including Prozac and Rifalin, are used as a first-level intervention to control behaviour in children and young people. Tranquillizers and anti-depressants are considered necessary treatment for people who have suffered serious physical injury or who are considered to be physically disabled.

The history of enforced lobotomies, sterilizations (as late as the 1960s in Sweden) and castrations recalls that medical surgery has also been used to control behaviour. Plastic surgery provides an example of the relationship between medicine and normality enforcement, in this case cosmetic. Surgery is used to eliminate perceived disfigurement, ugliness and abnormality. In the process it is clear that youth, normality and beauty are medically endorsed as components of human health. Medicine, aided and abetted by the pseudo-science of psychoanalysis, has proliferated a sequence of nonsensical categories for people whose behaviour differs from and upsets the norm: psychotic, schizophrenic, depressive, autistic, dyslexic, and so on. These categories are used to describe, stigmatize and treat behavioural, sexual, legal and even political (in the former Soviet Union, say) deviations from the norms of 'mental health'. Surgical and pharmaceutical interventions have been justified for such deviations. Even more radical solutions towards those perceived to have special needs have been adopted by several European states during this century: Mazower cites a Nazi text in a quotation which, by implicating the social priorities of the Third Reich, brings many of the themes of this book together: '"The construction of a lunatic asylum costs 6 million RM. How many houses at 15,000 RM each could have been built for that amount?" a maths school book asked children' (Mazower 1998: 99).

The people concerned in these pharmaceutical and surgical interventions – clients or victims – may also be subjected to waves of medical or para-medical 'counselling'. If your body or behaviour do not match medical and social 'normality', or even if you are in the process of enduring grief or unhappiness, then you are a candidate for counselling. Counselling reminds you subtly what the norm is, sympathizes with you for your failure to achieve it, instructs you how to handle your various inadequacies so as not to offend the normal, and how to conform in the future in as many ways as counselling considers possible for you.

Pre-natal screening, amniocentesis and ultrasound allow an increasing number of deviations from the medical norm to be recognized and diagnosed before birth. Where Downs Syndrome is diagnosed, abortion may be almost routine. The social consequence of such abortions is that there are now categories of people whose whole existence may be regarded as a medical mistake. Where children are fortunate enough to survive a condition where medicine would routinely terminate a pregnancy, how are they and others to regard the condition of their existence? Is human life only to be allowed to those whom medicine regards to be normal? Medicine has shifted the Nazi notion of 'purification' into the pre-natal phase where it apparently remains socially acceptable. As it is now possible to determine other characteristics, not least gender, at an early stage in pregnancy, the possibility emerges of the made-to-order baby, with all models that do not fit the specification peremptorily terminated. Genetic engineering, further, holds the possibility of the exclusive propagation of the scientific normal.

It may be argued that this is being selective in the aspects of medicine which are portrayed: that this is bad medicine but that most of European, modernist medicine is good (antibiotics, for instance, and miracle surgery). These two examples, of course, are not without their negative aspects: the degradation of antibiotics by their systematic use on farm animals in Europe and the United States; the routine and superfluous implementation of procedures such as tonsil-lectomies. The stress of the argument, however, is rather that if the aspects of medicine described and questioned in the previous two paragraphs are recogniz-able components, and actually rather significant components, of European, modernist medicine, then the whole edifice is flawed. This applies not only in relation to those perceived to be disabled but also in relation to those not (yet) so perceived. It is not being asserted that there is no such thing as health and sickness, nor even real disablement: rather it is insisted that, in western medicine, these concepts have become so associated with socially derived notions of normality, conformity, beauty and happiness as to render their continued imple-mentation as theory and practice prejudicial to the population at large and in particular to that segment of it perceived to be disabled.

It is in educational institutions, principally in universities and university hospitals across Europe, that this version of medicine is taught. It is important to emphasize, however, that this does not involve only university medical schools. Aspects of medicine are now taught to a whole range of would be para-medical professionals. Furthermore, medicine is seen to be one of the peaks of modernist science; it constitutes in the European Union one of the most desirable (and most difficult to attain) careers for those pupils and students most successful within education systems. In universities it is usually recognized as an elite subject; medical courses are characteristically longer than most others; those who teach on them are frequently paid at a higher level than other academics. One of the important functions of school science is to prepare young people for these medical and paramedical courses. Schools and universities not only teach modernist medicine, they also teach that this form of conceptualization, diagnosis and treatment is right, good and desirable. Other modes of diagnosis, aetiology and therapy (acupuncture, homeopathy, faith healing, herbalism and the like) are ignored, marginalized or denigrated. The actual construction of the school and university curriculum, then, underpins those conceptualizations, processes and institutions which have been so prejudicial to people perceived to be disabled.

A trend in much writing on special educational needs has been to criticize, rightly, the application of what has been called 'the medical model' in cases where it is deemed to be inappropriate (Sandow 1994). With regard to upsetting behaviour or to underachievement in school, for instance, it has been recognized that the use of medical terminology and procedures, far from assisting either understanding or intervention, is quite likely to be harmful to the people to whom they are applied. The potential for damage stems from the way these procedures both offer possibilities for stigmatization and also take the responsibility away from those most closely involved in working with the child or young person, almost always parents or carers and teachers. This chapter argues something beyond this: that it is not just the inappropriate application of the medical model which is the difficulty, but the whole medical model itself, and the European, modernist version of medicine and science which underpins it. Both as a version of scientific knowledge and as an institutionalized professional practice, this modernist medicine has been highly prejudicial to, among others, those children and young people perceived to have special educational needs.

In wider terms, of course, it can be seen as being prejudicial to everyone. As well as more general matters such as the morbid concern with health, beauty and fitness so prevalent in Europe, there are more specific issues which concern children and young people perceived to have special educational needs. The tendency to medicalize and stigmatize any form of deviation from the norm restricts everyone's version of what it is to be a human being. This restriction is compounded by the institutional arrangements of segregated schooling. Since so many children and young people in mainstream schools are not educated alongside their disabled peers, they do not learn about them, about their experiences or about ways in which they can collaborate with them. Their notion of what it is to be a human being falls within the highly restricted 'normality' of the medical model. The curriculum of the non-disabled is thus severely restricted, a restriction which, in its turn serves to enhance the credibility of the medical model.

## Knowledge Protocols: Stratification and Normality

The term 'knowledge protocols' refers to the way in which school knowledge is selected, organized, valued and assessed. Again there is a range of issues derived from the postmodernist critique of modernist knowledge which can be seen to be relevant to the education of children and young people perceived to have special educational needs. Underachievement is most frequently seen to be an attribute of the pupil or student concerned. It is a result of their (tautologically) perceived 'ability'. The victim is firmly blamed. But might this underachievement not be determined by the nature of the knowledge that is selected to be taught in schools and universities, or by the way in which it is organized? If a different aspect of knowledge were selected – co-operative and environment-enhancing, say, as against competitive and exploitative – or if it were organized differently – in an integrated, holistic way, for example, rather than in distinctly separated subjects – might not those currently perceived as underachieving be seen as successful, and an entirely different group of pupils be discovered to be underachievers? If this revolution were to be achieved might there not be predictable but different winners and losers in terms of 'race', gender or social class? Certainly there are cross-cultural differences in the status awarded to particular cognitive activities (Labov 1969). As discussed in Chapter Three, different groups have different notions of what constitutes knowledge. In considering the underpinnings of the prejudicial conceptualizations, processes and institutions of special educational needs, these issues remain to be addressed. The selection, valuation and organization of knowledge are considered in Chapters Two and Eight. The rest of this chapter is concerned with two knowledge protocols, those of assessment and intelligence, because these are the ones which are of particular negative relevance to children and young people perceived to have special needs.

Assessment – tests, examinations, checks on individuals' learning and learning patterns – is an important protocol for modernist knowledge. It allows educational institutions to recognize those who are succeeding and those who are failing. It allows for success to be rewarded and failure to be addressed. It allows rational, generalist decisions to be made instead of traditional particularist favouritism. Such decisions are easier to defend in democratic, open societies. The opening of the civil service in the United Kingdom to entrance by competitive examinations rather than by social sponsorship, in the mid-nineteenth century, is an example of the liberal, progressive policy-making favoured by the Enlightenment. Assessment, as a modernist protocol, opens, in the Napoleonic formulation, careers to talent; it provides an apparently rational filtering mechanism for successive levels of educational and professional promotion and allows for 'remedial' action for those seen visibly and measurably to be failing.

In England and Wales the implementation of the National Curriculum and its associated testing arrangements has recently industrialized the assessment process. All school-age children are assessed in at least three subjects at at least four points during their school careers on tests which are set, marked and, at least to the satisfaction of government politicians, standardized nationally. The result of this industry is that all school-age children can be calibrated, to the delight of journalists as well as politicians, according to their progress in at least three subjects. Data are available to compare them to the norm of their own school, of their LEA and of England and Wales as a whole, again in at least three subjects. The results of these assessments are regularly communicated to teachers and to parents or carers but, for the latter group, only in terms of their individual children. The results of other children in the class and school are supposed to be confidential, although conversations between parents or carers and children, as well as playground gossip by both parties, mean that the results, even for individuals, rapidly have some public currency. In terms of aggregate results for schools and for LEAs, these data are now routinely tabulated by government and media into league tables. The publication of the National Curriculum test results and of GCSE and 'A'-level grades are a regular media event.

These centralized assessment and publication arrangements set in motion at least two further educational processes, competition and stratification. These are not unforeseen outcomes of the 1988 legislation which introduced the National Curriculum; rather they are part of its clear intentions (Chitty 1989). The assessment sets child against child, teacher against teacher, school against school and LEA against LEA in a competition to get the highest scores. Those who formulated and adopted the Act believed in the positive social consequences of competition in its own right: it was a central component of their knowledge protocol (Bash and Coulby 1989; Coulby and Bash 1991). They considered that, in educational terms, these competitions would serve to raise standards of attainment.

With regard to stratification, the assessment arrangements highlight the successes and failures of each individual. Again this was seen as positive since the perpetrators of the Act were committed to an ideology of individual difference whereby some people are more 'intelligent' than others and thus are more successful in schools and universities, and thence in the wider society and economy. (A fundamental flaw in the current debate, or more accurately lack of debate, about the (un)desirability of mixed-ability teaching in secondary schools is that it utilizes the highly questionable concept of ability, 'intelligence', as if it were a self-evident truth.) This hierarchy, apparently reasonably enough, is reflected in subsequent life chances. The assessment arrangements make visible the hierarchy of success of pupils from a very early age and that, for New Labour as well as for the Tory enactors of the National Curriculum, is how life apparently is.

This theory of individual difference, with its reliance on a notion of generalisable intelligence or ability ('gifted pupils', 'the less able', 'remedial' and so on), is itself a product of modernity. The science of intelligence and its associated modes of calibration, not to mention fundamentally racist and sexist assumptions, were developed by psychologists working around the turn of the century (Simon 1971). It is an important component of the underpinnings of educational psychology in the United Kingdom, and elsewhere in Europe, today. More generally it informs the day-to-day assumptions, lexical frameworks and modes of judgement not only of politicians but also of many teachers and lecturers. The notion of intelligence is a centrally important knowledge protocol within modernist education.

The literature which exposes intelligence as a political rather than a scientific construct is familiar (classically, Kamin 1974). There is no such thing as intelligence. Human beings perform various intellectual and non-intellectual tasks with varying degrees of skill, according to their background, interests and enthusiasm. Very few people are successful in many areas. Very few fail in many. Educational institutions (and families) themselves play an important part in determining what level of interest and enthusiasm will be brought to bear upon a particular task. Equally important to this chapter is the insistence that what is seen to be 'intelligence', that is performance on a range of high status, high visibility tests, is itself dependent upon decisions made within other knowledge protocols. If knowledge had been differently selected, valued or organized then other and different pupils would have been the more successful in performance, that is, would have been more 'intelligent'.

The knowledge protocol of differential intelligence is itself taught and studied in European universities, especially within the discipline of educational psychology. Educational psychology, as a discursive strategy, attempts to schematize human difference in behaviour and performance, especially with regard to children and young people, and relate these to biological differences rather than to social and economic circumstances. This atomistic and naïve approach is currently being reinforced by rapid developments in genetics. Newspaper headlines that inform the public that homosexuality – to take but one absurd example – is genetically transmitted ensure that this knowledge protocol is more popularly available. People trained within educational psychology are often the professionals used by educational systems in testing for various perceived disabilities in terms of performance and behaviour. Their university credentials thus serve to legitimate the stigmatizing and segregative decisions that follow from these assessments.

The discipline of educational psychology has an even wider significance. In many countries in Europe it forms an important component of the education of teachers. Teachers' notions about behavioural conformity and about the differential 'intelligence' of their pupils are thus part of their professional preparation, legitimated by this area of university knowledge. Given the role of teachers in the processes of stigmatization and stratification described in this chapter, educational psychology is perhaps an essential professional legitimation. Certainly the reversal of these processes in the progress towards a more inclusive and comprehensive school system requires an entirely different philosophical framework from that derived from educational psychology (for a wide range of non-UK examples, see the essays in Daniels and Garner 1999).

One of the consequences of the assessment protocol is the stratification of children and young people. Central to this part of the chapter are the effects of stratification on pupils' lives. These effects can be summarized under three categories:

- the facilitation of labelling
- the legitimation of the existence of many of the categories of special educational needs
- the inhibition of inclusive education policies.

These three themes are examined in turn.

The assessment arrangements provide a ready label for each child: 'level oner' (the lowest attainment level in the English and Welsh national tests), 'not-very-good-at-maths', 'low ability' and so on. These labels carry the endorsement of government-sponsored judgement since they result from the apparently scientific and rational testing industry. It would be difficult for parents or carers to refute the accuracy of the government sponsored label and to insist that the child in question is actually rather good at maths, or that maths, indeed, covers a much wider range of global activity than is constrained in the school curriculum. Even less could they argue that the whole notion of ability is politically and educationally fraudulent and retrograde and should therefore never be applied to their child or, for that matter, to any other. More likely the parents or carers, and then the children themselves, accept the label from an early age and start living with ways of adapting to both it and its consequences. A critically important way in which they will adapt to the label is by not risking the failure that would be involved in attempting to challenge it. The child will accept the not-very-good-at-maths label, may even come to relish it, and thenceforth will feel extenuated from making too much effort in school mathematics. The result of this relaxation of effort, of course, will apparently be to make the judgement retrospectively correct. Such apparent correctness is likely to be repeated and further entrenched by each successive round of assessment.

The processes of self-fulfilling labelling have been described before, as have the ways in which pupils internalise the labels used about them (Hargreaves et al. 1975). The apparent fulfilment of the label appears to legitimate its use, proves that it is 'true'. By internalizing the label, the subject of it gives the whole process a further level of authenticity. When a pupil accepts the 'not-very-good-at-maths' label, this has consequences for subsequent educational and almost certainly economic success. But failure at school and in the workplace can be made to seem fair and correct: it is justifiable because 'I was not-very-good-at-maths'. This then places the burden of responsibility on the individual child and removes any blame or indeed possibility of positive action from educational institutions, their processes and personnel. In internalizing the label the subject defends her/himself against the hurt of educational, social and economic failures and their associated stigma. The assessment system is seen to be just and subjects can acknowledge their place in a hierarchy with the minimum amount of stress. 'I failed at school because I was not-very-good-at-maths but I am happy about what I did. It is nobody's fault but my own. But that's the sort of person I am' (that is basically okay). Instead of the label then being identified as one of the causes of educational underachievement, it is taken on, by both agents and victims alike, as 'proof' that the system is just and that everybody is happy. It is for children perceived to have special educational needs that these processes have particular power. Those consistently at the lowest end of the performance scale in the school or national tests will have labels applied to them even more pernicious and enduring than 'not-very-good-at-maths'. In segregative school systems, such as that of England (see OFSTED 1999 for the latest situation), such labels can all too often be transformed into institutional arrangements ('remedial' classes, schools for children with moderate or severe 'learning difficulties' and the like) whereby pupils are subjected to a restricted curriculum and a negatively selected peer group.

As well as the consequences for individual pupils, national curriculum and assessment arrangements and the associated testing regimes, often masquerading as diagnostic screening, function to legitimate whole categories of perceived special educational need from 'low attainers' groups via 'remedial' classes to 'moderate and severe learning difficulty'. The differential performance on the national tests proves, to both agent and victim alike, what those inculcated in the discipline of educational psychology already know: that people have different natural abilities. The tests, by definition, ensure that there is always a category of children at the lowest level of this stratification. They demonstrate that this category of pupils 'needs' (for of course this whole notion of special educational need should itself have been in scare quotes from the very start) a different form of educational provision, preferably segregated from the rest of the age cohort, and ideally in a separate institution out of sight and out of mind.

And in the process of legitimating one form of special need all the others too are brought into more concrete conceptual and institutional existence. Once there is a 'science' which taxonomises children according to their perceived ability/need/disability, then other forms of difference – blindness or a tendency to upsetting behaviour, say – can all be brought in as other sub-categories of this rational and ameliorative science.

The category of special educational needs is entirely one of ascription. The need is in no sense derived from the individual social or economic need of the child or young person under scrutiny (for a square meal, for instance, or to be removed from a physically and sexually abusing environment). The need is derived from the disciplines of medicine and educational psychology, which position individuals along scales of normality with regard to behaviour, performance and appearance, and are highly intolerant of those who fall at the bottom end of their self-perpetuating taxonomies. More crudely, the need can be derived from the institutional arrangements which these professionals will deem appropriate. A headteacher desires that a troublesome, underperforming child be removed from mainstream schooling; an obliging psychologist discovers that the child has a low 'IQ'; the child is sent to a segregated school for slow learners (various euphemistic designations). As part of this process the child is discovered to need specialist teaching away from the excitements of mainstream schooling. The provision that the system intends to impose is legitimated as what the child needs. The fact that the children and young people subjected to these processes are almost exclusively working-class (Ford et al. 1982) and disproportionately black (Tomlinson 1981, 1982) is hidden in the ameliorative, pseudo-scientific processes which conceal themselves in the discourse of meeting individual needs. Special educational needs in too many countries of Europe have been used as a way to stigmatize and exclude particular groups (Westwood 1994).

Romania provides a further example of the racial aspect of segregated special provision, as well as the ways in which provision made often with the best of intentions may, in the event, serve to further disadvantage some children and groups. Romania has made a separate provision for Roma children to allow them to have intensive help in their education and then return to the mainstream. Although this provision is theoretically for all impoverished children it is actually almost exclusively Roma who attend. Although they are meant to be reintegrated into mainstream school this rarely happens. Furthermore, the nature of the provision, the curriculum followed and the training of the teachers is identical with that associated with the special education of children with severe learning difficulties (McDonald 1999). Two things then happen: segregationist education of Roma children is legitimated on the basis of their special need; all Roma children, and indeed Roma people, can all too easily be identified with children with severe learning difficulties. Lest this paragraph be seen as the comforting western stereotype about the unfortunate Romanian gypsies, a recent press report indicates a parallel situation in the Czech Republic, where Roma children are fifteen times more likely than Czech children to be placed in schools for 'the mentally retarded'. Roma rights campaigners are taking the Czech Ministry of Education to court over the issue in a move which parallels American black activists' struggle to break down the segregative provision for black children thirty years ago (Glass 1999).

England and Wales has a rigidly segregationist tradition for the education of children perceived to have special needs (Bash et al. 1985) and the wider conse-quences of the assessment arrangements introduced by the 1988 Act have been further to inhibit the development of inclusive schools. The published test results are not the record of an abstract competition: there is a real and tangible prize. It is assumed, with only some degree of accuracy, that parents and carers will use the published test results, the league tables, when selecting schools for their children. Since funding now automatically accompanies pupil numbers, by a parallel provision of the 1988 Act, schools are, in the main, anxious to recruit as many children and young people as they possibly can. This is not only a test of popularity; it is the way of ensuring continuing employment for teachers and buoyant budgets for academic activities. Primary and secondary schools are therefore looking more and more cautiously at pupils who are likely significantly to reduce their aggregate test scores. It is of course the more 'successful' (in terms of the tests) schools that can afford to be thus discriminating (and discriminatory). The other schools must take what pupils they can find. Those children and young people who are scoring at the very bottom end of the tests, however, are increasingly unattractive to all schools. This applies even more to those pupils whom schools consider to be likely to impede the scores of other children due to the extent of their upsetting behaviour. The assessment arrangements actually constitute a disincentive, within the education system as a whole, to the creation of inclusive schools. Instead they function to perpetuate the demand, from teachers, headteachers and even parents or carers in mainstream schools, for exclusion and for segregative provision.

It is European knowledge systems and their associated protocols, at least as much as the embedded institutional arrangements which they underpin, which are responsible for legitimating and reproducing prejudicial attitudes towards children and young people perceived to have special educational needs. Prejudice and stereotyping are processes intrinsic to the modernist knowledge system. This has been recognized and challenged by increasing numbers of groups that the knowledge systems attempted to reduce to victims, inferiors, patients, perverts, to name just some of the characterizations involved. The challenge on behalf of children and young people perceived to have special educational needs is taking place within and beyond schools and universities. As well as developing a critique of modernist knowledge, this challenge needs to develop and publicize accounts of non-prejudicial ways of constituting, organizing, legitimating, sharing and evaluating knowledge and knowledge systems (Coulby and Coulby 1995). That is to say, it will need to develop new, non-prejudicial knowledge protocols that can lead to a more inclusive understanding of what it is to be a human being.

## Discussion Questions

1   Is the category of special educational need entirely one of ascription?
2   How might the concept of a least-restricted educational environment alter the schooling of children perceived to have special needs?
3   What concepts may be used to replace those of intelligence and ability?

4   What are the theoretical and policy links between this chapter and chapter four? Are there identifiable common features between those groups who are disadvantaged by school and university curricular systems?

## Further Reading

Kamin's demolition not only of IQ but of the whole notion of intelligence is a way of thinking which could be exceedingly helpful to teachers: Kamin, L. J. (1974) *The Science and Politics of IQ*. New York: John Wiley. The educational issues which this raises concern grouping in primary and secondary schools as well as inclusion. This is an area of sharply overlapping discrimination.

Perhaps the most accessible of all Foucalt's books is *Madness and Civilization: A History of Insanity in the Age of Reason* (1967). London: Tavistock. It provokes a profound re-thinking of what it is to be sane as well as of the political and social reasons for exclusion and incarceration.

For a recent, international account of the politics and possibilities of inclusion see: Daniels, H. and Garner, P. (eds) (1999) *World Yearbook of Education 1999: Inclusive Education*. London: Kogan Page. This excellent volume interrogates the various, interrelated ways in which educational institutions can discriminate against individuals and groups.

# 7    Knowledge and
       Warfare

## Introduction

To say that Europe invented warfare and that warfare was its principal bequest to the rest of humanity would be an exaggeration, but not a large one (Anderson 1988; Best 1998; Kiernan 1998). Since the emergence and consolidation of the European states, warfare – both against their own populations and against the armies and navies of neighbouring states – has been a characteristic of their history. The period of imperialism spread this systematic engagement in war and conquest, along with its associated European military technology, to the rest of the world. The twentieth century in Europe has been one of apparently unceasing warfare. Europe has twice this century dragged the world into its wars (Mazower 1998). The progress of the Wermacht from Berlin to Stalingrad and back in the company of the Red Army marks the single most murderous, inhuman and destructive episode in human history (Overy 1998). It is against such episodes and such a history that Europe's claim to be the birthplace and repository of civilization must be tested.

In Chapter Three it was argued that there was a tension between the heterogeneous nature of the populations of European states and the state-controlled homogeneity of the content of their school and university curricula. This chapter takes the argument further. It contends that there is a link between what is taught in schools and universities in particular states of Europe, and elsewhere, and the likelihood of them pursuing policies of warfare either with regard to their own populations (internal) or that of other states (external). The curricula of schools and universities are capable of exacerbating or reducing the propensity of a state to engage in warfare. This chapter examines in turn many of the curricular components which are particularly involved in these processes: language policies, history and cultural studies, religious education, scientific research and development programmes, military training, training in conformity. In doing so it revisits, from a pointedly different angle, some of the themes which have been examined in earlier chapters. The link between knowledge and warfare allows the dissonance between demographic heterogeneity and state-controlled or approved curricular systems to be heard in its most clear form.

Much of this chapter makes links between curriculum content and the encouragement of nationalism, xenophobia and racism. It is the contention of this chapter that one of the consequences of this link can be actual warfare. Ignatieff writes:

> It was in Vukovar that I began to see how nationalism works as a moral vocabulary of self-exoneration. No one is responsible for anything but the other side. In the moral universe of pure nationalist delusion, all action is compelled by tragic necessity. Towns must be destroyed in order to liberate them. Hostages must be shot. Massacres must be undertaken. . . . Everyone in a nationalist war speaks in the language of fate, compulsion and moral abdication.
>
> (Ignatieff 1994: 32)

This language is learned, among other places, in the schools and universities of Europe.

## Foreign and First Language Policies

In the case of foreign languages, first, and on national linguistic diversity, Greece provides an example. The historical background here is the population exchange of 1923, long-term bad political relations with Turkey over issues such as Cyprus and the Aegean Islands, opposition to the formation of the state of Macedonia (FYROM) and wider Balkan hostilities. Greece has long claimed that its treatment of its Turkish minority, largely in Thrace, ought to be the example followed by Turkey in the treatment of its Greek minority. Certainly in Thrace there are no official restrictions on the use of Turkish either in schools or in mosques. The educational treatment of Slav speakers, Albanians and Vlachs, elsewhere in Greece, is less positive. To take the latter example, Pettifer reports that officially, as there are no recognised ethnic minorities in Greece, Vlach is not today used in schools, although before the war there were many Romanian-sponsored schools in the Pindus villages. Consequently many Vlachs feel that, as they have never done anything to destabilize the Greek political system in terms of separatist or nationalist ambitions, they should have more educational recognition of their language. Although a small group whose linguistic distinctiveness may be denied by their neighbours, the Vlachs retain a strong sense of identity. But Athens is unresponsive 'and many independent observers feel that the whole issue shows the over-centralised and inherently authoritarian Greek educational and cultural establishment at its worst' (Pettifer 1994: 186–7). As well as national diversity Greece also has considerable urban diversity, for example the relatively recent but numerically significant Polish population in Athens. The linguistic position of this minority, who are often illegal immigrants without citizenship, is even weaker than that of the Vlachs (Lazardis 1996; Romaniszyn 1996).

In terms of language, schools and universities in Europe frequently fail to reflect the linguistic diversity of their regions, which might have facilitated communication, understanding and tolerance between groups. They prefer instead to adopt a perceived international language as their chosen second language. In much of Europe and the world this language is increasingly English. In Thrace children may be taught Turkish, but the other minority languages of Greece – Albanian, Vlach, Macedonian – are invisible in schools and universities. The idea that Greek-speaking children should be taught Turkish as a foreign language rather than English would be seen in Athens as academically and politically unthinkable. The language policy of the schools and universities reflects the domestic and foreign policy of the state. This policy is not without belligerence. The state wishes Greece to be Hellenocentric; other national identities within the state are not to be encouraged. It is at odds with its Balkan neighbours (except Orthodox Serbia) and context, preferring through its membership of the European Union and NATO to contextualize itself within a European and western set of relations (see, for example the essays in Constas and Stavrou 1995 and Allison and Nicolaidis 1997). At best, this language policy does nothing to inhibit or reduce political tensions in the eastern Mediterranean.

Latvia provides an example of a state in transition. Not surprisingly Russian was abandoned as a foreign language in Latvian-speaking schools soon after independence. Furthermore, the Russian-speaking schools, and especially universities, are rapidly being transformed so that Latvian is the language of instruction. The state has gone through a process of reversed linguistic asymmetry: Russian was in a dominant position and Latvian subordinate in education and society under the former Soviet Union; now Latvian is in a dominant position and Russian subordinate. In the Latvian-speaking institutions the first foreign language, formerly Russian, is now English. There are economic reasons for this as Latvia struggles, with some success, to enter international trade. But the change in educational policy is also motivated by political and cultural considerations as the language of Soviet imperialism is cast off and the language of the (implied free and democratic) west adopted. Unfortunately, however, almost half the population of Latvia is Russian-speaking. Furthermore Russia itself is a neighbouring state and important trading partner. The language policy of the Latvian education system is likely to restrict communication both among citizens of the state and with its largest and most powerful neighbour. Combined with citizenship laws which made it very difficult for Russian speakers to obtain passports and voting rights, this policy exacerbates political tension between Russia and Latvia. From Moscow the perception is all too easily that of Russian people and their language being oppressed by a state which also blocks their access to the Baltic Sea and the rich port of Riga. The 1998 Referendum which approved citizenship rights for Russian speakers perhaps presages a less belligerent curricular policy.

The actual linguistic diversity of European states is, as was demonstrated in Chapter Three, an exceedingly complex pattern. It represents a source of cultural

and economic capital available to these states. In the spread of global languages –
Russian until 1991 and English and Chinese still – these cultural resources are
increasingly at risk. This risk is exacerbated by those school and university
curricular policies which enforce the learning of global languages and neglect
those of the state's nations and cities. Furthermore, a language is not only a mode
of communication, but also embodies and represents a culture. To have access to
one's neighbours' language is to be able to understand something of their
religion, literature, philosophy, law and science.

In the first-language and literature curriculum, the teaching of a set canon of
texts remains a feature at school and university in almost all states of Europe. In
some countries this canon is well-established and authenticated. In countries
which have recently emerged or re-emerged, the establishment of the national
literary canon is an important element in state building, as was shown with the
case of Latvia in Chapter Four. These canons tend to be national in their structure
and nationalistic in their content. They identify rich cultural traditions and
achievements with the geography of a particular state. They neglect the literature
of other nations within the state, Scottish, say, or Welsh. They make no attempt
to encompass the urban diversity which now characterises the populations of so
many European states. The actual texts within the canons are not without
xenophobia and chauvinism. Indeed actual warfare is all too often a characteristic
of the canonical texts: *The Iliad*, the Icelandic, Norse and German sagas, *The Song
of Roland*, *Orlando Furioso*, *Henry V*, *The Lusiad*, *the Poem of the Cid*, *Le Rouge et le
Noir*, *War and Peace*.

> Come the three corners of the world in arms,
> And we shall shock them! Naught shall make us rue
> If England to itself do rest but true!
> *(King John*, v, vii, 116–118)

*The Mountain Wreath* is a nineteenth-century Serbian epic poem about the
defeat of the Serbian army at the Battle of Kosovo in 1389. With other epics on
the same defeat it has helped to make the Battle of Kosovo an integral part of the
national cultural heritage: 'In all European history it is impossible to find any
comparison with the effect of Kosovo on the Serbian national psyche' (Judah
1997: 30). The poems and the mythologized version of history together are used
within and outside educational institutions to reproduce a highly nationalistic
consciousness: or, as Judah concludes, after his analysis of the Croatian and
Bosnian wars, 'Serbian history was misused to do harm to others and give power
to the few' (ibid.: 310).

Cultural products are themselves closely linked to warfare both as cause and
effect. They provide the patriotic and jingoistic rhetoric which helps prepare
populations for war. They display warfare in terms of glory, national expansion or

survival, heroic individualism and self-sacrifice rather than as plain greed and carnage. Schools and universities are one of the main institutions through which this link between culture and warfare is mediated and reproduced.

## History and Cultural Studies

Turning to history, Greece can again be used as an example. Considering the image of Europe presented in the compulsory textbooks of Greek elementary schools, Flouris discovered that the references 'do not portray the image of Europe conceived by the EU member states. On the contrary, students are exposed to the concept of Europe via wars, conflict etc' (Flouris 1995: 115). Similarly, looking at social studies set books across the levels of secondary schooling, he discovered that, contrary to the stated aims of the teaching of history in Law 1566/85, young people in Greece become acquainted with other countries through the teaching of wars (Flouris 1996a). The teaching of Hellenic history in Greek schools tends towards the formation of nationalism, since it lacks cosmopolitanism and there are few references to other ancient civilizations except the Roman (Massialas 1995). This centralized curriculum, with its state-endorsed compulsory textbooks, follows values which are also espoused by a largely traditionalist teaching force. Since it is the other Balkan countries in particular which are presented in the context of war and invasion, during the Byzantine period and the war for independence (Massialas and Flouris 1994), then the question of the relationship between the compulsory school curriculum and the policy of the state, with regard both to its non-Greek citizens and its Balkan and Mediterranean neighbours, is again one which falls to be addressed. While it might be going too far to suggest that this curriculum stimulates hostility and warfare, it certainly does remarkably little to encourage reconciliation and peace. Identities inscribed with this level of nationalism and xenophobia are a necessary, if not sufficient, condition for warfare.

The discussion in Chapter Three suggested that modern states have tried, with varying degrees of success, to identify themselves with nations. By a process of religious and linguistic intolerance across many centuries, the state of France has almost succeeded in disguising itself as the nation of France (Braudel 1989, 1990). In other cases an artificial national identity has had to be manufactured: the United Kingdom has been less successful at persuading the English, let alone the Scots, the Welsh and the Irish, that they are *British* (Grant 1994, 1997). Similar difficulties face the governments of Spain, Belgium, Italy and Romania. The national tensions in these countries are strong and enduring. Some states have broken beneath these tensions: the Soviet Union, Yugoslavia, Czechoslovakia and, as recently as the early 1920s, the United Kingdom. To return to the example of Greece, the attempt there is to identify the modern state, via Byzantine Orthodoxy, with the city-states of the fourth century BC and thus with

Hellenic civilization (Psomiades and Thomadaki 1993). Expansionary policies in the past and belligerent postures in the present are legitimated inside a knowledge system which sees the idealized Greeks as the cradle and repository of European civilization and which focuses on neighbouring states only in the context of warfare. In attempting to bury the state's recent history of internal and external warfare and conflict beneath a homogenous Greek and Orthodox identity, the curriculum only exacerbates tensions with internal minorities and bordering states. While the educational reform in Greece implemented in 1998 (Law 2525/1997) explicitly addresses the curriculum and assessment of the *enieo lykeio* (Zambeta 1999), it does nothing to address its xenophobic content.

The history curricula of schools and universities are ethnocentric in two parallel ways. First, they concentrate on the triumphant emergence of, or ascent to world power of, a particular state. Thus the Golden Century is central in the Netherlands, the Risorgimento in Italy, the industrial revolution and imperial period in England and Wales. Despite aspirations towards European studies or world history, the overwhelming concentration in history teaching in most European states is on national events. (Norway provides a welcome exception here, see Royal Ministry of Education 1997). Regional histories, that is, those of other nations than that with which the state seeks to confuse itself, are forgotten or deliberately hidden in such systems. The history of Scotland remains concealed from pupils in the schools of England and Wales, and indeed from those in Scotland itself. Only by permitting manifold versions of the school history curriculum has Spain come close to reconciling the intensely felt national passions through which its many histories are codified (Mackey 1997). Equally lost in such curricular systems are globally important events which took place beyond the state's boundaries: the Spanish invasion of Latin America or the Thirty Years War are neglected topics in the National Curriculum of England and Wales, as the rise and fall of the Japanese Shogunate is across Europe.

The second way in which school and university history curricula are ethnocentric is in their tendency towards overt nationalism. They place undue importance on events, personalities, discoveries, processes and achievements local to one state. They exaggerate the importance of one state in the history of the world.

The history curriculum necessarily pays explicit attention to the subject of warfare. As in all curricular areas, there are choices to be made here. Should history be social and economic as well as political? How are the lives of women to be regarded in school and university history? The decision to teach political and military history is likely to mean that other forms and versions of history are marginalized. Once military history has become central, the influence of the state is certain to be all the more firmly felt. The former Yugoslav school curriculum taught of the defeat and exploitation of Serbia not only by Turkey but also by other constituent nations of the state (Rosandic and Pesic 1994). It taught of the world's indifference to Serbia's suffering. (To point this out is by no means to deny the magnitude of this suffering (Judah 1997)). It encouraged hatred for other groups in the state and disdain for international opinion. In times of war, or in near-war conditions, this tendency in the history curriculum may be exacerbated. In primary schools in the southern part of Cyprus there is a subject called, 'I learn, I don't forget and I fight for the freedom of my country'. While at one level this is absolutely understandable, at another it gives a stark example of an uninhibited relationship between curriculum and warfare.

Of course to ignore conflict and warfare in history can be as much of a political message as to concentrate on it. In the United States the history of the slave trade and slavery is receiving grudging acknowledgement in schools and universities, but the genocide of the Plains Indians is a matter which is still largely ignored (Lamawaima 1995). The history curriculum at school and university in Germany and the United Kingdom is faced with similar dilemmas. To what extent should children and young people in the United Kingdom learn about the English conquest and subjugation of Wales, Scotland and Ireland; about the slave trade and its importance in the generation of the wealth which fuelled the industrial revolution; about the less attractive side of the imperial adventure, the Opium Wars, say, or the treatment of native people in Australia? In what ways can young people in Germany be exposed to the history of the Holocaust (Supple 1993) and of the nature of the Second World War on the Eastern Front? That the curricular systems in both states largely shy away from these matters betrays the tendency to hide and deny these components of their history rather than a decision to concentrate on other aspects of historical studies or on more peaceful epochs.

## Religious Education

Religious education remains in many countries a cornerstone of xenophobia. Again the links between religion and warfare are manifold, and school and university curricula are only one of the instruments of their mediation and reformulation. In Northern Ireland and in Cyprus, as well as in the former Yugoslavia, religion remains one of the major fuses for actual conflict. Nor is this link maintained only within the subject of religious education. Even in those states such as France, where education is secular, the history and literary presentations of crusades and jihads assist in the maintenance of the link between religion and warfare.

As described in Chapter Four the survival of religious institutions and curricula in so many states in Europe and elsewhere is one of the triumphs of traditionalism over the Enlightenment project. These traditionalist survivals are all the more remarkable in that they occur in societies which are overwhelmingly secular. It is widely believed that, during the nineteenth century, in states such as the United Kingdom and France the state gradually took responsibility for education away from the churches (Archer 1984). In the case of the United

Kingdom, the Netherlands or Belgium, this underestimates the extent to which the churches were able to infiltrate the emerging state control of education and retain a strong traditionalist presence.

The strong part played by religious authorities in many states reinforces and reproduces one strand of pluralism whilst ignoring and denigrating another. In the Netherlands, Catholic and Protestant groups are able to administer schools and polytechnics. Educational institutions provide a site where their cultures and practices can focus, develop and reproduce. On the other hand, this source of strength is frequently denied to other groups, though Muslim groups have now succeeded in establishing their own schools (Dwyer and Meyer 1995). In the United Kingdom Catholic, Protestant and Jewish groups have all been able to obtain substantial state finance for their primary and secondary schools for many years. However, only recently, with the coming to power of New Labour, have a few Islamic school succeeded in obtaining such backing (Lepkowska 1998). The idea that the compulsory daily act of worship in England and Wales should be Islamic would be anathema to policy makers even with reference to those schools in London where every child is a Muslim. Though some rights of religious recognition have been achieved in these schools which have a predominantly Islamic population (Sarwar 1993), a secular, multi-faith approach is the best that can be tolerated, with rare exceptions even in religiously diverse urban areas. The secular curriculum and ethos of the state schools of France continues to come into conflict with those Islamic pupils and students who wear traditional religious costume to school.

Control of educational institutions by religious authorities, and religious education as an aspect of the school curriculum, have rarely been elements of European education systems which have served to increase tolerance and respect for plurality. Rather, they have served to allow particular cultural groups to maintain an undue influence over education, often at the expense of other, less powerful groups. The Greek Orthodox church continues to use schools and teachers in its active campaigns against what it considers to be heresy (Karaflogka 1997). Religious intolerance is one of the capacities which facilitates the waging of war. In Chechnya and Tibet, on the other hand, it is secularized education in schools which is one of the ways in which war is conducted by other means.

While the importance of traditionalism is appropriately being stressed, there is an aspect to the survival of religious elements inside education systems which is a component of modernity. In most cases the religion favoured in schools and universities is that favoured by the state itself: Orthodox in Greece, Catholic in Ireland, Protestant in Norway, generically Christian in England and Wales, secular in France. These religions are not only those which obtain arbitrary state approval; they are those of either a majority of the population or of its most powerful groups. Furthermore, they are part of the legitimation in which the state presents itself. Education is only one of the policies whereby the state does this through performing in ostensibly religious (or secular) ways. Others include policies on contraception, abortion, divorce, blasphemy and, less overtly, immigration. Thus the teaching or practice of religion in European schools and universities also provides instruction to children and young people on the nature of the state to which they belong. Even in countries such as England where religion has long since ceased to be an important component either in society or in the identities of the bulk of the population, religious education and worship in schools teaches children that the state ('the nation', 'the culture', 'the people') is Christian. While part of the intended function of this is doubtless to engender an enhanced sense of social solidarity and cohesiveness, it is actually selective with regard to the religion it endorses, even within the strange category of generic Christianity, and is thereby socially divisive. If the state legitimizes itself as Christian and seeks to reproduce the identity of its citizens within this religious strategy, then those of other religions – and to a lesser extent, those of no religion (Rudge 1998) – will be seen as outsiders, potentially as non-citizens. Conflicts between the white, Christian nation and outsider groups such as Islam are not accidental but intrinsic to the state's religious strategy in education.

Furthermore, similar polarizations between insiders and outsiders occur between those educated in the religified curriculum of the state and inhabitants of other states with other religions. The anti-Islamic climate prevalent across Europe needs to be acknowledged as at least in part produced by the religious strategy of states in educational institutions. In Europe, not least in schools and universities, the adjective Islamic and the nouns extremist or fundamentalist are far too readily linked. Non-pluralistic religious education has created an ignorance of the nature of Islam, its contribution to human history and civilization and the current unhappy situation of many of its believers, in Bosnia and Tower Hamlets as well as Palestine and Kashmir. This ignorance and prejudice is not unrelated to the practice of actual warfare, as is shown by the contrast between the lethargy of the European Union military powers in intervening to save a Muslim population in Sarajevo and their speed and enthusiasm to intervene against an Islamic state in Iraq. The Gulf War example provides an opportunity to make explicit the extent of the argument in this part of the chapter. It was not the reinforcement of anti-Islamic prejudice in the schools and universities of Europe and the USA which brought about this war. The safety of the west's oil supply was a far more tangible reason. However, the existence of anti-Islamic prejudice made it easier for European populations to accept the necessity and rightness of the war. Religified curricula were by no means a sufficient cause of the war; they were, however, a necessary component of its initiation and continuation. Anti-Islamic prejudice is an important plank in European xenophobia. It is a central component in internal and external conflict. Far from seeking to reduce this prejudice, the school and university curricula in many European states, including those ostensibly secular, have functioned to encourage and perpetuate it.

## Scientific Research and Development Programmes

The science taught in schools and, especially, universities is explicitly linked to warfare. The key test here is, what do pupils and students do with science? To the extent – still minor – that young people actually use the science they have learned, it is within a limited range of occupations. School science prepares young people to be medical doctors or to be research scientists. While, for the latter group, much of this research itself concerns medicine and pharmaceuticals, another large tranche of it consists in the development of military technology.

During the Vietnam war, the United States military was faced with the difficulty that the victims of napalm attacks could actually brush the inflammable substance from their burning flesh. It was necessary to find a type of napalm which could not so easily be removed. Children progress from learning at primary school that oxygen is necessary for combustion to assessing ph values at secondary school and then to be young people who investigate the qualities of flammable substances at university. They may subsequently obtain successful employment as researchers, quite possibly in the same or another university, where they can develop ways in which napalm can be made more adhesive to the human skin. Scientific research, much of it actually conducted in universities, is funded by armament manufacturers and other providers of military technology. A well educated science 'community' working in fully equipped laboratories and with access to the latest learned journals is an indispensable component in the ability of states to wage modern, high-tech warfare, or to provide the materials whereby other states can thus dispose of their tax revenues. Scientific and technical education provides the tools of war.

The United States, the European Union, Japan and those other countries which consider themselves to be, or aspire to become, 'smart states' do so because they know that knowledge, as shown in Chapter Five, is increasingly the most valuable trading property in the global economy. Knowledge itself can be traded; it can also assist in the manufacture of other products which because of their technical superiority can command a high price or a large market or both. Pre-eminent among such products are armaments and military technology. From land mines, the low-tech export of countries such as China, to the Hawk jets which British Aerospace provided to the Indonesian government for the domination of the civilian population of East Timor, the arms trade is predicated on the provision of school and university science. Enlightenment science perceived itself to be a liberating agenda which would set humanity free from centuries of ignorance and superstition. In its most tangible and pre-eminent, current manifestations – trident submarines, cruise missiles – it has become, via education and politics, one of the main tools of domination and aggression.

Science is also part of the ethnocentric and xenophobic knowledge that serves to facilitate the practice of warfare. In this respect medicine and mathematics may also be brought into the argument which covers the trajectory of the objective knowledge developed by the Enlightenment. These were the areas in which Europeans were most certain that their knowledge was superior to, and indeed truer than, that of other, less enlightened people. The neglect of acknowledgement to non-European achievement and influence in science, mathematics and medicine is remarkable. Western science and mathematics are taught in European schools and universities as the one true way. There is no acknowledgement, for instance, that the Western number system is derived from the Arabs or the concept of zero from India (Joseph 1992). There is little or no attention paid to non-western number systems. There is little attention given to other ranges of scientific explanation or methodology, or to other conceptualizations of human health and the ways in which it may be maintained. This ethnocentric narrowness of focus has two important consequences: first, the nature of western science is limited and unnecessarily constrained in its access to the variety of international wisdom: second, because of the spectacular achievements of western science, not least in warfare, it forms the core component in the epistemological superiority complex so characteristic of Europeans.

Nor are the actual activities and social functions of science, in terms of technical, exploitative interventions in the natural world or of the development of the global armoury, investigated. In medicine, discussed from another perspective in Chapter Six, the pharmaceutical and surgical paradigms are paramount. Despite the popularity and proliferation of alternative therapies in the United States and the European Union, these receive little acknowledgement in the university medicine curriculum. Invasive surgery and post-Freudian psychoanalysis are medical science; acupuncture and homeopathy are magic. More importantly, European medicine teaches, to patients and clinicians alike, a notion of human health predicated upon illness and professional intervention. It sees health only in terms of its opposite and treatment as individual and atomistic. It has little conception of health as a component of all life, no matter the degree of clinical or aesthetic impairment, as something generated in interaction with family, community and the awareness of living creatures and landscapes. In this way science and medicine have placed constraints on the way in which Europeans live, their access to a wider conception of health, and their understanding of what it is to be human.

While mathematics, science and medicine may not be curriculum areas which evidence petty state nationalisms, they are part of a wider western xenophobia which finds it difficult to acknowledge achievement outside its own paradigm and which, in particular, is loath to recognize the cultural, scientific and political achievements of Africa and Asia. In facilitating the belief that real, true, hard knowledge originates only in the west, the teaching of science, mathematics and medicine facilitate the economic and, if necessary military, domination of other parts of the world.

## Military Training

Military training is itself actually a component of much of education throughout the world. The most extreme current example is Venezuela, where President Chavez (himself a former paratrooper and leader of a military coup) has recently decreed that all children must be given military training. In both primary and secondary schools children are to be instructed in military strategy, weapons handling and issues of national sovereignty (Gamini 1999).

In Europe and the United States, at the higher education level, are training centres, academies (Keegan 1993) and elite institutions such as Sandhurst, West Point and St Cyr, where young people, mainly but not exclusively men, are taught the most effective ways to kill and maim the maximum number of other servicepeople and civilians in the shortest amount of time and at the least expense to the taxpayer. Many countries, such as England and Wales, have service training corps as part of schooling. Interestingly, these are overwhelmingly prevalent in the fee-paying public schools where they take the form of officer training corps. The reproduction of the United Kingdom's officer class remains a function which these institutions explicitly maintain. Young people, again mainly young men, practise dressing up in military regalia and shouting and marching about in schoolyards. They go on adventure weekends when they camp, play war games and experience the thrill of handling real military technology. At this stage they are not usually allowed to kill or maim anybody but they are instilled into the rituals (competitive camaraderie, social licence) and discipline (obedience to authority, nationalism) of military behaviour.

But military training does not need to be quite so explicit as this. A good deal of standing up and saluting the flag, or shouting and marching about in yards, is done in schools and universities in Europe without any explicit reference to military activity. Collective acts of assembly or worship often involve national or military insignia or reference. Playground games follow the dramas and personalities of the state's latest military adventure. Often toys and equipment provided by playgroups, schools or other benevolent authorities encourage and facilitate the emulation of military behaviour from a very young age (Dixon 1990). In this respect play and toys form one of the earlier gendering experiences of European children. It is boys in particular who are given guns, model military aircraft, action men and military uniforms as appropriate play equipment. The development of commercial ICT has spawned flight simulators, military games and conquest scenario games in various formats from hand held machines through to pentium technology. Again it is overwhelmingly boys who are encouraged to take an interest in such products.

Physical education and sports accustom children and young people to the disciplining of the body so central to military service. In England and Wales physical education used to be referred to, revealingly, as drill. Such acitivtes help to establish the values of teamwork, co-operative competition and *esprit de corps*. The

99

very format of invasive team games mimics the eighteenth-century battlefield. It cultivates a fitness and athleticism which is one of the necessary components of militarism. This athleticism also has its ideological dimension: toughness and ruthlessness as well as muscularity are internalized as masculine virtues. The internalization of military virtues is made essential for those who will not ultimately be servicepeople as well as for those who will. Obviously compulsory military national service for all in many European countries assists with this ideological process of the legitimation of warfare. Physical education and team sports further encourage a competitiveness within and between institutions which readily leads to the frenzied chauvinism of national tournaments in sports such as rugby or football, or even the Olympic Games. As the Duke of Wellington remarked, the Battle of Waterloo was won on the playing fields of Eton.

## Training in Conformity

The ways in which schools reproduce patterns of authority and conformity are familiar themes of the sociology of education (Grace 1978). In some cases this has been linked to the perceived requirements of a workforce within the capitalist system (Bowles and Gintis 1976). It is more obviously, as well as more generally, linked to the requirements of a militarized population. Although now abandoned in the United Kingdom, conscription remains a feature of the lives of young people in many European states, including those as ostensibly peaceful and stable as the Netherlands and Switzerland. In transitional states such as Russia, conscription, though profoundly unpopular, is, with education, one of the foundations of nation building. In order for a population to accept the astonishing infringement of personal liberty represented by the disciplines of conscription, and for young people to consent to it with little or no hesitation, earlier forms of social control are clearly essential. To the extent that schools and universities help to produce an obedient, conformist population, they assist in ensuring people's consent for, and indeed participation in, the act of warfare.

Mass warfare and mass education are both aspects of modernity. The *levee en masse* and the products of the industrial revolution transformed warfare from an activity of small professional armed forces into total war which engages entire economies and populations. Educational institutions became in the nineteenth century the chosen means by which the philosophy of the Enlightenment was transmitted and developed. While the link between the two processes were rarely explicit, they were able to coexist in harmony if not symbiosis. The schooled, young English volunteers who walked so readily over the top on the first day of the Somme offensive, the scientifically educated Germans who developed the gas and the bureaucratic-industrial system necessary for the death camps, the technical self-sufficiency which ensured the rapid re-industrialization of the eastern Soviet Union and provided the materials for the Red Army's break out from the Volga, all hang together as part of a society in which education, material production and warfare are the three central components, whatever the political ideology.

Among the issues considered in the final chapter is the postmodernist critique of enlightenment knowledge. As this critique of knowledge gathers force in the educational discourse, it may be that different forms of education, if not of warfare, may emerge. While a postmodernist curriculum is far from identifiable in any European state, the knowledge system on which it might be based is now visible. Postmodernism acknowledges not only the international contribution to western civilization but also that western knowledge systems themselves must be placed within an international context of which the west is but a part. Postmodern knowledge systems recognize the importance of women in the formation of history, culture and knowledge. They recognize the wealth of different knowledges, sciences and cultures which are in dialogue and conflict. Such systems are intrinsically international in a way in which western traditional and modernist systems have failed to be. School and university knowledge have been vital elements in the reproduction of ethnocentrism and warfare. It is possible that they could be just as powerful elements in their reversal and ultimate elimination. The postmodernist critique and its version of a pluralistic, contested, manifold, provisional knowledge may offer the most positive alternative for curricular systems. It may serve to begin to erode ethnocentrism and provide a more humane version of science, and thereby to diminish the likelihood of warfare.

Warfare is ongoing in Europe: civil strife in Corsica, the Basque country and Northern Ireland; genocide and ethnic cleansing and associated NATO responses in Bosnia and Kosovo, post-imperial adventures such as Iraq or the Malvinas. Wider conflict waits ever dangerously in the wings as evidenced by the Russian response to the NATO intervention in Kosovo, or Greek and Turkish sabre rattling over obscure Aegean islands. In Europe, the joke has it, countries go to war not to control the future but to control the past. There is a depressing accuracy to this. The main place where the past – controlled by the victors – is reproduced is in the school and university curriculum. It is then both the beginning and ending of warfare. Despite this, modern states will rarely go to war unless their tangible political and economic interests are threatened. Even then the nationalism and xenophobia supplied by the school and university curriculum may be a necessary, though not sufficient, element in the mobilization of the population, especially those called upon to fight, in the acceptance of warfare. In states thrown by transition into outbreaks of traditionalist fervour, notably Serbia, the school and university curricula, along with religious institutions and the state-controlled media, may become the main strands in the formation and reproduction of xenophobic nationalism capable of undertaking any military extremity or barbarity. Where schools and universities have taught nationalism and hatred they are not innocent of their involvement in European warfare.

Wilfred Owen wrote this reproof to Horace and this advice to educators from the Western Front in 1917. The narrator cannot escape dreams of a comrade who has been the victim of a mustard gas attack.

> If in some smothering dreams you too could pace
> Behind the wagon that we flung him in,
> And watch the white eyes writhing in his face,
> His hanging face, like a devil's sick of sin;
> If you could hear, at every jolt, the blood
> Come gargling from the froth-corrupted lungs,
> Obscene as cancer, bitter as the cud
> Of vile, incurable sores on innocent tongues, –
> My friend, you would not tell with such high zest
> To children ardent for some desperate glory,
> The old Lie: *Dulce et decorum est*
> *Pro patria mori.*

## Discussion Questions

1   How is warfare presented within texts that comprise the literary canon of school and university curricula? Does this differ between states?
2   Is the chapter right to identify science as the core component of the European epistemological superiority complex?
3   Was Wilfred Owen right to blame the suffering of his comrade on the teaching of Horaces's poetry?
4   How might this chapter have been different had it focused on peace instead of war?

## Further Reading

For a reminder of the full horror of war, try: Overy, R. (1998) *Russia's War*. Harmondsworth: Allen Lane.

To relinquish any anglocentric views about the role of the UK in warfare, see: Kiernan, V. G. (1998) *Colonial Empires and Armies*. Stroud: Sutton.

Of the works cited in this chapter which attempt to chart the relationship between education and warfare, the Rosandic and Pesic collection provides a convincing case in the extreme example of former Yugoslavia: Rosandic, R. and Pesic V. (eds) (1994) *Warfare, Patriotism, Patriarchy: The Analysis of Elementary School Textbooks*. Belgrade: Centre for Anti-War Action MOST.

# 8 State Knowledge and Identity

## Marxism, Postmodernism and Educational Policy Formulation

When I give lectures in my own institution or as a visitor, the question that I am most frequently asked is: 'What *should* be in the school and university curriculum, then?' I have become resolute in resisting this temptation towards the normative. This final chapter will show a similar reticence. It is not concerned with specifying an ideal-typical school or university curriculum for either Europe or anywhere else. Rather it reformulates the interrogations and critiques of existing curricular systems made in the preceding chapters. It does this largely from a position which may be characterized as that of postmodernism (from the huge literature, see, for example Ellin 1996; Jameson 1991; Lyotard 1984; Young 1995b). This position itself inclined me strongly towards normative evasiveness. The postmodern critique has disrupted grand narratives, undermined academic taxonomizing, playfully rejected any attempt at 'one true way' to truth. Indeed its lack of specificity may partly account for its still surprisingly low impact on curricular formation at school level (though educational writing now proliferates, for example, Arnonowitz and Giroux 1991; Coulby and Jones 1996; Cowen 1996; Smith and Wexler 1995; Usher and Edwards 1994b) or, within the more positivistic subjects, at university level.

The use of the first person at the outset of this chapter has perhaps already alerted the gentle reader to a shift from the expository to a more self-conscious mode. I fear that this must continue a little longer as I seek simultaneously to explain the extraordinary relationship between postmodern theory and curriculum formation, and to extenuate my own reluctance to engage in curricular formation.

First, the story so far. Postmodernism is not a movement, it is more a climate of opinion. Emerging from such diverse fields as French epistemology and American architectural studies, postmodernity can be identified as an intellectual strand, if not a movement, from at least the early 1970s. (This may be seen as distinct from a social condition of postmodernity. Castells' argument, discussed in Chapter Five, that changes in the mode of technology and the organization of global capitalism are taking society into a new epoch is rather different from the intellectual movement of postmodernism (Castells 1996, 1997, 1998).) During the 1970s and 1980s other critiques of conventional wisdom, derived from anti-sexism and anti-racism became associated with postmodernism. Further active groups and writers, such as those concerned with the handicapped or committed to reducing homophobia, could also be seen as part of this intellectual climate. The tendency to conceptualize society in intercultural and international terms is another discernible trend, as also is the critique of science which emerges from an environmental assessment of the effects of contemporary technology. These political or social movements each involved a critique of existing knowledge, both in academic institutions and in society. Indeed, it is these added accretions of critique which make postmodernism particularly attractive to those trying to understand curricular systems. Postmodernist sociology, philosophy and critical theory *per se* can often seem sterile and remote from the tangible concerns of more conventional social science. This is an important issue but fortunately not central to the argument of this chapter. The contention that follows is simply that within the critique generated by those working in the framework of postmodernism there is an exceedingly insightful approach to understanding the curricula of European schools and universities.

It is difficult to recall the remarkable dominance which intellectual Marxism had in many subjects at university level in Europe and, to a much lesser extent, the United States in the early 1980s. In artistic criticism, economic theory, sociology and even educational studies (Sharp 1980), Marxism, if not the dominant discourse, was at least a significant and long-standing intellectual position. In the period between 1989 and 1991, as the Berlin Wall came down, Ceaucescu's troops fired on demonstrators in Timosoara, and people across the Baltic States linked hands, it became abundantly clear that state socialism was intellectually as well as politically discredited. There was a rapid, if largely tacit, re-assessment of intellectual Marxism (Derrida 1994). Some few struggled to make yet another historical reformulation of Marxism. Many looked for a different intellectual position. Disillusioned with one failed ideology, with a grand narrative which had been dramatically discredited by history, they were particularly attracted to the scepticism and relativism of post-modernism. In many cases, across many subject areas, yesterday's Marxists did an elegant, and often unnoticed side-step and became today's postmodernists (see, for instance, the difference in emphasis of Bash, Coulby, and Jones 1985 compared to Coulby and Jones 1995). Currently at university level, in both Europe and the United States, the theories and lexicon of postmodernity are everyday currency in literary and artistic studies, philosophy and sociology. They are even emerging in educational studies themselves. As described in the previous chapter they have made little impact on one of the areas of their most persistent critique, science. Nor have they had any influence on the formation of school curricula. Why not?

In some ways this may be answered by examining the complex relationship between educational policy makers and wider intellectual movements. To keep the argument within bounds, this section will focus on their relationship to educational research itself. It is not that policy makers are resistant to the findings of educational research. In many ways, in England and Wales at least, they might be seen as being overly credulous. A pilot study on the teaching of literacy is judged to be successful in a handful of schools and the DfEE, disregarding any possible halo effect, announces a National Literacy Strategy making the scheme compulsory for an hour a day in every school in the land. Nor are policy makers oblivious of practice in other states. South Korea scores remarkably well on mathematics tests in international comparisons. Pupils in South Korea are taught from the front as a whole class and not in small groups. So policy makers across Europe and the United States persuade or compel teachers to adopt whole-class teaching. Similarly, at the beginning of the TEMPUS programme in the early 1990, one of the university disciplines in which the then state of Czechoslovakia characterized itself as being in need of western assistance was, astonishingly, art history. This has been well characterized by Cowen as 'cargo cult comparativism' (Cowen 1998).

But policy makers are selective in the kinds of educational research which they adopt and legitimate. The dramatic success of the schools-effectiveness research programme clearly demonstrates the nature of their preferences. With readily identifiable targets — homework for all children, headteachers who are good managers, a potted plant in every school foyer — effective schools research is irresistible to policy formulators. It readily fits into their preferred discursive strategy of standards (see Chapter Five). They have been happy to commission it, finance it, publicize it and adopt it. This has not been the case with the intellectual programme of postmodernity either in terms of educational discourse or as a wider movement. On the contrary, and not only in the United Kingdom, there has been a strong tendency to redefine the actual nature of educational research so that it is *only* about school effectiveness. If research does not assist teachers to deliver the curriculum, or, more elegantly, children to learn, or, more politically, schools to raise standards, then it simply cannot be research. If it is not research then it cannot influence policy, should not be funded, ought not to be taking place in universities. Any educational research more abstract than how to teach phonics is likely to trigger the book burning tendencies of the curricular centralists.

Of course much is left unquestioned in this restricted notion of educational research:

- What exactly is the knowledge which is being learned?
- In what matters of cognitive development are standards to be raised?
- Can the relationship between teacher, pupil and knowledge in any way be characterized as 'delivery'?
- What is the relationship between background, learning, maturation and identity development?
- Do the structures of school curriculum and assessment (knowledge protocols)

have any bearing on economic and social reproduction in terms of the life chances of individual children and young people?
• Do they have a bearing on social reproduction in terms of the state as a whole?

In short at least three things are left out in this attempt to restrict the nature of educational discourse: knowledge, children and society.

Of course this book itself is part of the educational discourse, and hence the self-consciousness at the opening of this chapter. It would certainly not qualify as educational research in the dangerously restricted definition currently favoured in the UK. It belongs to sub-sets of the educational literature – curriculum studies, sociology of education, international education, comparative education – currently profoundly unfashionable in the UK and the USA, yet re-emergent in states such as Portugal, Spain and Greece. But even when this form of educational research was apparently more popular, it was still almost completely without influence on educational policy. This book attempts to bring curriculum studies in Europe into closer contact with mainstream social theory on such matters as transitions, warfare and the knowledge economy. Nevertheless, it inevitably belongs to a long strand of literature. And it is this particular strand which, since at least *Knowledge and Control* (Young 1971), policy formulators have found particularly easy to ignore and now apparently would prefer to silence altogether.

There are two different sets of reasons for this, which may be examined in turn: first, the acute political sensitivity of the content of the school, in distinction from university, curriculum; second, the nature of the theorizing which has been espoused by people writing in curriculum studies. The issue of political sensitivity is relatively straightforward. For most people within education, let alone outside, the curriculum is very much a taken-for-granted matter. Most people believe what they are taught at school; furthermore they believe that what they are taught at school is what everyone should be taught at school. To suggest that school knowledge is erroneous, or that some quite different matters might be taught, or that knowledge could be formulated or assessed differently, is to fly in the face of the profound process of socialization embodied in compulsory schooling. Policy formulators and politicians share this taken-for-granted, traditionalistic attitude to school knowledge. Once they are shown the possibility of alternative curriculum formation, however, they are quickly alert to what they perceive to be a social, or indeed political, threat. If the school curriculum were to be radically shifted away from the characteristic lies and nonsense habitually taught across Europe and the United States, then there would be the possibility that whole tranches of the population would gain insights into matters which politicians consider should not concern them: the international arms trade, say, the use of non-state-taxed drugs, or the levels of pollution in the North Sea and the Mediterranean. For politicians these are dangerous matters. If the mode of the music changes, may not the walls of the city fall? It was the move towards the implementation of anti-sexist and anti-racist curricula in urban areas of England and Wales which helped to bring about the draconian National Curriculum and the abolition of the ILEA. The purpose of centralization was precisely to restrict curricular debate. Greece in 1998, seeing itself in an apparently threatened international situation, left unchanged the traditionalistic content of the school curriculum, when otherwise systematic educational reforms were implemented (see Chapter Seven).

The relative openness of the university curriculum to radical ideas and approaches is perhaps partly associated with the freedom of ideas on which many European and American higher education systems pride themselves. It must also, however, be associated with the economic position and expectations of both lecturers and students. It appears that students can be exposed to the most blood-curdlingly radical theories in the safe expectation that they will contentedly trot off into well-remunerated posts in banking, marketing or the arms industry at the end of their courses. Nevertheless, as was shown in Chapter Five, this openness has meant that universities have been able to respond to rapid technical change and to position themselves as prominent players in the knowledge economy, whereas schools are in danger of lapsing into the child-storage units which Castells (above) stigmatizes.

Turning to the second reason for the unpopularity of curriculum studies writing among policy makers: the nature of curriculum studies theorizing. This has been characterized by a high degree of political explicitness and a low degree of ready accessibility. Curriculum studies has been at least as much influenced by the two trends of Marxism and postmodernism identified above as the rest of educational discourse. In both cases there is an explicit political agenda: the first concerned with differential knowledge and achievement between social groups and the utilization of school knowledge as a mode of social control; the second prone to criticize Francocentricism, Eurocentricism or sexism in curricular content. At the same time neither Marxism nor postmodernity, given the complexity of their theories, can be celebrated for the lucidity or transparency of their proponents' prose style. That one is labelled after an apparently discredited political enemy and the other after an incomprehensible oxymoron in no way helps maters. Politically suspect and conceptually arduous, radical curriculum studies can be ignored or denigrated by policy formulators in favour of the safer and more conducive discursive strategy of school effectiveness. In this failed interaction between theory and practice, the wider questions about children, knowledge and society are ignored, at least in the case of schools, and the traditionalistic and modernistic curriculum remains increasingly anachronistically in place.

## Postmodernism and Curriculum Structure

While the above section goes some way to explaining my reluctance to offer normative curricular guidelines, a further reason lies in the nature of the postmodern critique itself. Previous knowledge systems, associated with the Enlightenment, science, say, or Marxism, would characteristically include:

- a preferred area of subject knowledge, the link between society and the economy or the nature of the physical world
- a particular methodology, dialectical materialism or falsification
- a particular truth claim, the power of the proletariat or fact.

At the centre of postmodernism is a profound distrust of these matters. It prefers to expose and undermine canons of knowledge or study. It is methodologically as well as culturally relativistic: it does not see one way to truth or even the possibility of one truth (Feyerabend 1978a, 1978b), examining rather the repertoire of discursive strategies. Obviously, then, it would be difficult for anyone working within this critique to start specifying curriculum content at either school or university level. Some of the people working in curriculum studies in an earlier generation (Hirst, Peters, Tyler but, interestingly, not Dewey) were themselves the kind of system builders criticized by postmodernism (Dewey 1944; Hirst and Peters 1970; Tyler 1949). The only extent to which it is possible to lapse into the normative, then, is perhaps to specify that curricula at all levels must entail critique and must seek to reveal rather than conceal social, cultural and epistemological assumptions. Beyond this it is much easier for postmodernism to be clear about the interestedness of particular curriculum content and the way it is embedded in wider social and cultural assumptions than to specify with what alternative (presumably socially and culturally neutral or many-sided and presumably unembedded) content might be essayed.

This of course is not a negligible achievement: it sweeps away a lot of the lies and nonsense; it offers at least critique as subject matter; it offers many-sidedness as a criterion for inclusion of further subject matter. To be tempted to go beyond this is to allow personal prescription, a preference for peace over warfare, say, to masquerade as scripted by cutting-edge theory.

To use the critique of postmodernism to interrogate curricular systems begs one further question. The way in which knowledge is organized in Europe into school subjects and university departments is itself a taken-for-granted epistemology. While the several sections of this book do indeed examine particular subjects, the very framework and structure of the school and university curriculum in Europe remains organized and understood in traditionalistic and modernistic ways. Much of the playfulness attributed to postmodernist writers is derived from their unwillingness to accept epistemological categories or conventional distinctions between so-called high and low culture. Discussions of science involve aspects of style and taste, learning from Las Vegas is a sociology as well as an approach to urban planning. Once identity formation and reformation are fronted as important topics, the scale of argumentation necessarily oscillates between the widest environmental and social constraints and the most particularistic aspects of aesthetics or autobiography.

Parallel to the discussion of the knowledge economy in Chapter Five, it is in universities – where postmodernism largely originated and where in some departments it has made considerable inroads – rather than in schools that the structuring of knowledge has undergone some modest reformulation. Interdisciplinary degrees and the more general move towards modularization have allowed for programmes of study and research less constrained by the old departmental certainties. Open Universities have proliferated in Europe and beyond, though not yet in centralized Greece. Developments in information and communications technology (ICT) are likely only to facilitate this process, as masses of information along with the tools to manipulate them become increasingly more available between as well as within departments. Open and distance learning is explicitly favoured by the European Union, as well as by state governments, for its perceived accessibility as well as cost-effectiveness. In schools more topic-centred approaches to curriculum, associated with Dewey, have been swept away in the USA, the UK and the Netherlands in the face of South Korean mathematical prodigousnesss, though not in Italy or Scandinavia. Centralized curricula can be more easily designed, enforced and policed when they are shaped around subjects. A compulsory curriculum which encouraged teachers and pupils rigorously and exhaustively to follow their own intellectual interests across whatever subject boundaries would be something of a contradiction in terms. The current relative openness of universities to ICT developments and to the impact of the knowledge economy is likely to stretch to breaking point this difference between the way in which knowledge is structured at schools and in higher education.

Any discussion of the postmodern critique of curricula which concentrates on subjects, then, is in danger of shooting its own fox. The glory of the morning, after all, is to go tallyhoing and stirrup-cupping over hedges, gates and ditches, charging after the discursive insanity which separates History from Politics, Sociology from Economics and Science from Morality. The postmodernist critique implies a radical restructuring as well as revision of European knowledge.

## State-Enforced Knowledge

At school level, the further concern which arises from the postmodernist critique is that of the compulsory and universal nature of so many European curriculum systems. If knowledge is infinite, many-sided, tentative, contested and relative, why are children and young people legally compelled to learn a highly partial version of one fraction of it? Furthermore, why should that small fraction be the same for all children and young people within a given state? This section now addresses these two issues.

Previous chapters have stressed the role of schools in 'nation-building', the task of disguising states as nations. National language, culture, history and geography are taught to all citizens in the attempt to shape identities towards a commitment to the institutions and behaviour patterns of a particular state. Schools are institutions for nationalizing identity. Central governments take a keen interest in this process at particular historical points. The post-Soviet era in Eastern Europe has been such a period. In universities as well as schools, an older generation of teachers – of Russian, say, as well as history and economics – could not be trusted. Central government control of curriculum was seen to be essential to prevent it falling into the wrong political hands. Marxism and dialectical materialism have been swept out of the school and university curriculum from the five new *lander* of Germany (Wichmann 1998) to Bulgaria. The disappearance of the Russian language has been almost as far-reaching and rapid. Educational policy has thus been an essential tool in the reformulation of national identity as being liberal, capitalist and western-inclined. The National Curriculum in England and Wales was introduced at a contrasting time of transition (Coulby, Cowen and Jones 2000) . Part of the economic transition of the UK in the 1980s involved much closer links with the rest of the European Union and the signature of the Maastricht Treaty. At the same time, the fabric of the United Kingdom was itself in jeopardy through warfare in Northern Ireland and the strength of nationalist parties in Scotland and Wales. National identity was perceived as being under threat from both Europeanization and regionalization. Furthermore, the multicultural population of the English cities led to racist conceptualizations of an endangered British culture and identity. The centralized and nationalistic National Curriculum was a political attempt to inscribe traditionalistic English identities on this conflicted and transforming society.

A second consideration in the homogenizing of school curricula concerns assessment. It is not only the political programme of educational standards which demands frequent testing, it is also that of cost effectiveness. Perhaps as a component of the marginalization of schooling, taxation to fund expenditure on education has become increasingly unpopular in the USA as well as in many European states. In order to justify such expenditure politicians have wished to show that taxpayers are getting value for money. National level tests are necessary to reveal whether standards are rising (because of sound political intervention) or falling (due to poor teaching). They also allow a coefficient to be constructed based on how much is spent in a particular school and what the levels of assessment results are. In this way a spurious value-for-money league table can be constructed. In order for standards and value-for-money projects to be maintained there must be assessment at various stages of schooling at a state level. In order for such assessment to take place there must be a compulsory, homogenized curriculum. Of course the results of such assessment can also lead politicians into the appreciably less complacent areas of national comparators discussed earlier in this chapter.

The more conventionally Marxist response to the question concerning compulsory, homogenous curricula would refer to the need to reproduce the workforce for advanced capitalism (Castells 1977) and to the tendency to correspondence between the knowledge and practices of school and those of the workplace (Bowles and Gintis 1976). Chapter Five suggested that, in the case of schools, though appreciably less so for universities, the curriculum was becoming remote from the workplace needs of the knowledge economy. It seems that the political motivation in the formation of knowledge protocols has become more important than the economic. That states should place more importance on the inscription and control of identities than on ensuring future economic prosperity would seem to fly in the face of sound democratic judgement as well as Marxist theory. Yet in periods of transition, crisis, or, particularly, warfare, it is precisely this preponderance of the political which has been seen in Europe in the twentieth century. (Overy (1998) describes the way in which the would-be internationalist Soviet Union reformulated itself as Mother Russia following the German invasion.) The reproduction of nationally inscribed political conformity may actually be more important to European states than the reproduction of labour power. An alternative explanation is that schools are becoming marginal institutions. The employers of the knowledge economy are looking to universities, further education and specialist institutions for the workforce they need. This is hard to reconcile with massive state expenditure on schooling across Europe. However, the low funding and scant political importance given to schooling in some non-suburban areas of the United States might presage the further marginalization of this level of education.

## Language, Curricula and Identity

In considering why all school pupils should be taught the same knowledge, it is again necessary to question the structuring of the curriculum. The tendency towards subjects has been examined earlier in this chapter. What is at issue here is which subjects are selected and why they are the same for all pupils for so many years of their schooling. The unquestioned centre of curricular systems in European states is the endorsed language or languages. Literacy in the state language/s gives access to substantial economic and political opportunities, as well as widening the mechanisms for identity formation. But is this literacy taught at the expense of the national or family language? This is decreasingly the case for national groups in Europe but increasingly the case for many urban groups.

Furthermore, the way in which the state language is taught reveals the knowledge protocols at work behind curricular homogenization. For all the recent stress on grammar and spelling in the teaching of English in England and Wales, there is scarcely any attention paid to the origins of the language. To know that English is derived from French and German (Anglo-Saxon) would certainly assist in its acquisition but it might betray foreign influences at the very core of national and individual identities. Similarly, Romania perceives itself to be an island of Romance in a sea of Slav. The nationalistic Romanian myth is of a continuity of settlement between Roman Dacia and the contemporary state. A monument to Romulus and Remus and their lupine nurse, donated by the Italian government, in the Transylvanian (and preponderantly Magyar-speaking) city of Cluj testifies both to its Romanianness and to the classical origins of this identity. The teaching of Romanian in schools and universities is therefore equally shy of examining linguistic origins. That the first examples of writing in Romanian are not found until the sixteenth century is as little examined as the systematic romancifying of the language in the nineteenth century.

The compulsory, homogenized teaching of state languages is as much about the control of identity construction and the reproduction of cultural nationalism as it is about providing political and economic access. This argument can readily be made with regard to the curricular inclusion of history, geography, literature, art, music and dance, but it is essential to see it also in that cornerstone of education, the state language. Literacy is a double-edged sword: whilst it gives political access, its acquisition allows political control of identity formation. Individuals struggle with varying degrees of success against the political inscriptions of identity. To learn a language is to learn an ideology; words come from nationally structured cultures not from dictionaries (Hodge and Kress 1993; Lodge 1990). 'You taught me language and my profit on it is I know how to curse', jeers Caliban, the renaissance, romantic, postmodernist brute, at Prospero.

Foreign language is an important component of the knowledge protocols in Europe, especially in those countries where English is not the first language. State bilingualism and its role in schools in countries such as Finland and Belgium was discussed in Chapter Three, where the ineluctable spread of the teaching of English was also queried. However, the teaching of English as a first or, more rarely, second foreign language is widespread in Europe in schools and universities as well as in the many flourishing language schools. In Greece, Romania and Latvia, English is seen as a key skill in acquiring political power, economic success and cultural authenticity. The choice of which foreign language to enforce on school pupils is highly political. The economic and commercial prevalence of English is evident from banking to air traffic control. But this is not the only reason for the decision to adopt English. As Spain and Portugal emerged from dictatorship, English has gradually replaced French. (Catalan, Gallician and Basque have also acquired ascendancy as discussed in Chapter Three.) This was not because French was seen as the language of tyranny or because the UK and the USA had replaced France as the important trading partner. English, as well as its pragmatic value, embodied aspirations towards democracy, liberty and prosperity associated with the USA. When English replaced Russian on the curriculum of Estonian and Latvian speaking schools, this was much more consciously a rejection of (not least linguistic) imperialism. English as the language of capitalism, as well as democracy and of international culture in contrast to Russifying insularity, was eagerly embraced.

That this would limit communication among the citizens (or non-citizens) of Riga and Tallinn as well as with their major trading partner (which remains Russia) was unimportant compared to the immense political message encapsulated in the adoption of English. Mazower provides a humbling historical analogy: 'Student enrolment for German classes at the Berlitz in Paris shot up from 939 in 1939 to 7,920 two years later; numbers taking English plummeted' (Mazower 1998: 145).

The complexity is that when people outwith England – Ireland may be a moot point, Scotland and Wales are certainly not – learn English, they are acquiring so much more than a means of communication. In learning English the associated view of English and American culture, history and institutions is almost invariably positive: adulation of Shakespeare or American intervention in the Second World War. In learning English one learns from and learns about English cultural products, from Newton to the Spice Girls. The very mode of learning will be from UK and American cultural sources: texts, literature, newspapers and magazines, the BBC, Hollywood movies, British-Council-selected costume drama videos, English-language pop music. Even a smattering of English will provide some access to, and some market for, these cultural products. The UK is the world's largest exporter of books and 40 per cent of London publishers' sales come from export. Similarly three-quarters of UK records are produced for export (Lash and Urry 1994).

But these are not the only products that can sail in the glorious wake of the English language. English is increasingly the language of advertising, despite government attempts to restrict this in Poland as well as in France. With the films and the pop songs come the more tangible cultural products of Coke, Macdonald's, Microsoft, of shopping in Regent Street and visits to the RSC. English gives access to understanding English adverts often for American or English (not only cultural) products. That this access is educationally derived gives these products another layer of status. The teaching of English and the spread of these commercial products are mutually reinforcing activities.

There is a political as well as a cultural and commercial message embodied in English. In learning English, people elsewhere in Europe inevitably learn about American and English political institutions: about elected presidents and constitutional monarchs; about democracy, the Land of the Free and the Mother of Parliaments. Certainly, it is only necessary to count the number of democracies left extant in Europe in, say 1943, to be cautious about undermining the democratic discourse, even though it is centred on the UK and the USA. Nevertheless, there is a danger that, in associating (in some cases newly found or refound) democracy with the language and institutions of the UK and the USA, these two states are provided with a legitimacy which goes beyond the integrity of their institutions. As the UK increasingly plays Robin to the USA's Batman in military interventions from Iraq to Kosovo, it is important that these two states do not lever for themselves an inappropriate level of political legitimation. As triumphant, if not successful, capitalism is established in Eastern Europe, it is important that the associated spread of

English does not eliminate the languages and discursive strategies within which a more humane, egalitarian and environmentally sustainable economic system might be envisaged (Orr 1992a, 1992b).

In Europe, racism cannot be separated from nationalism and wider forms of xenophobia (*contra* the contributors to Rattansi 1994). Linguistically structured identities are central to these forms of xenophobia and the sites where these identities are produced and reproduced are school and university curricula. The discourse of curriculum studies then has something critically important, if highly unpalatable, to explain both to educational policy makers and to mainstream sociologists. Schools are not marginal in the reproduction of individual and social identities. They remain a mechanism whereby the state can inscribe its values on each generation. If these values are to change away from nationalism and intolerance, away from chauvinistic and hostile particularism, away from stratification and exclusion, then the traditionalist and modernist school curriculum needs to be transformed. While the university curriculum is slowly and partially engaged in this transformation, schools remain play-pens for the reproduction of Europe's atavistic, self-destructive knowledges.

What then should be in the school and university curriculum? In concluding, the danger is to advocate curricular utopianism and to associate this with either decentralization or postmodernism. A shift in this direction might certainly provide benefits both in terms of identity formation and social and economic solidarity. A relaxation of centralized homogeneity might allow for the development of interdisciplinary studies and the revival of forbidden areas of knowledge. The wider teaching of sociology and economics might allow greater access to understanding, and thereby potentially transforming, those global processes which lead to such gross inequalities. A knowledge of the languages, cultures, sciences and economics of non-Europe might provide access to attitudes to humanity and nature which are less exploitative and potentially more sustainable than modernist science and technology. The learning of a variety and plurality of languages could lead to less constrained and nationalistic identity formation, as well as multiplying possibilities for intercultural and international communication and trade. A scepticism about grand narratives would be of assistance in constraining the momentum of science and capitalism. The cultivation and preservation of individual multiple identities and wider social heterogeneity might increase the possibilities of movement and exchange. In this exchange knowledge is itself the central issue. The enhancement of its heterogeneity may well be associated with economic prosperity, as well as with social and international tolerance.

## Discussion Questions

1  Why is the school, rather than the university, curriculum a matter of such political sensitivity?

2   The chapter characterizes school and university curricula as 'lies and nonsense': to what extent is this exaggeration?

3   What are the other sites of identity production and reproduction apart from curricular systems?

4   What *should* be in the school and university curriculum, then?

## Further Reading

I am cautious of recommending readers into the paths of postmodernity without a guide. Before attempting to navigate Lyotard, Derrida and Jamieson, those coming from education, therefore, might try: Coulby, D. and Jones, C. (1995) *Postmodernity and European Education Systems: Centralist Knowledge and Cultural Diversity*. Stoke on Trent: Trentham.

For an up to date, international account of higher education and the ways systems are responding to the exigencies of quality control, see Cowen, R. (ed.) (1996) *The World Yearbook of Education 1996: the Evaluation of Systems of Higher Education*. London: Kogan Page.

# References

Aldrich, R. (1988) *The National Curriculum: an Historical Perspective*. London: Institute of Education.

Allison, G. T. and Nicolaidis, K. (eds) (1997) *The Greek Paradox: Promise vs, Performance*. Cambridge, Mass. MIT Press

Althusser, L. (1972) 'Ideology and the Ideological State Apparatus'. In B. R. Cosin (ed.), *Education: Structure and Society*. Harmondsworth: Penguin.

Anderson, M. S. (1988) *War and Society in Europe of the Old Regime*. Stroud: Sutton.

Appadurai, A. (1990) 'Disjuncture and Difference in the Global Cultural Economy'. In M. Featherstone (ed.), *Global Culture: Nationalism, Globalisation and Modernity*. London: Sage.

Archer, M. (1984) *Social Origins of Educational Systems*. London: Sage.

Arnonowitz, S. and Giroux, H. A. (1991) *Postmodern Education: Politics, Culture and Social Criticism*. London: Routledge and Kegan Paul.

Ascherson, N. (1996) *Black Sea: the Birthplace of Civilisation and Barbarism*. London: Vintage.

Bash, L. (1998) 'Continuity and Change: The Question of Jewish Ethnic Identity'. In K. A. M. and M. G. Spillane (eds), *Education and The Structuring of European Space*: 333–7) Athens: Seirios Editions.

Bash, L. and Coulby, D. (1989) *The Education Reform Act: Competition and Control*. London: Cassell.

Bash, L. and Green, A. (eds) (1995) *World Yearbook of Education 1995: Youth, Employment and Education*. London: Kogan Page.

Bash, L., Coulby, D. and Jones, C. (1985) *Urban Schooling: Theory and Practice*. London: Cassell.

Best, G. (1998) *War and Society in Revolutionary Europe 1770–1870*. Stroud: Sutton.

Blunkett, D. (1999) *Challenge to Invest in Human Capital* (Press release) London: Department for Education and Employment.

Bowles, S. and Gintis, H. (1976) *Schooling in Capitalist America*. London: Routledge and Kegan Paul.

Braudel, F. (1989) *The Identity of France*. (Vol. 1). London: Fontana.

Braudel, F. (1990) *The Identity of France*. (Vol. 2). London: Fontana.

Bryant, G. A. (1997) 'Citizenship, National Identity and the Accommodation of Difference: Reflections on the German, French, Dutch and British Cases'. *new community*, 23 (2): 157–72.

Buchan, D. (1998) 'First Steps Towards Integration'. *Financial Times* 21 October: Survey III.

116

Byrne, G. and Mckeown, P. (1998) 'Schooling, the Churches and the State in Northern Ireland: a Continuing Tension'. *Research Papers in Education: Policy and Practice* 13 (3): 319–339.

Carr, R. (1980) *Modern Spain: 1875–1980*. Oxford: Oxford University Press.

Castells, M. (1977) *The Urban Question: A Marxist Approach*. London: Edward Arnold.

Castells, M. (1989) *The Informational City: Information Technology, Economic Restructuring and the Urban-Regional Process*. Oxford: Blackwell.

Castells, M. (1996) *The Information Age: Economy, Society and Culture* (vol. 1: *The Rise of the Network Society*) Oxford: Blackwell.

Castells, M. (1997) *The Information Age: Economy, Society and Culture*. (vol. 2: *The Power of Identity*) Oxford: Blackwell.

Castells, M. (1998) *The Information Age: Economy, Society and Culture*. (vol. 3: *End of Millennium*) Oxford: Blackwell.

Chitty, C. (1989) *Towards A New Education System: The Victory of the New Right*. London: Falmer.

Chitty, C. (1992) *The Education System Transformed: A Guide to School Reforms*. Manchester: Baseline.

Chitty, C. and Simon, B. (1993) *Education Answers Back: Critical Responses to Government Policy*. London: Lawrence and Wishart.

Chouliaras, Y. (1993) 'Greek Culture in the New Europe'. In H. Psomiades and S. Thomadkis (eds), *Greece, the New Europe and the Changing International Order*. New York: Pella Publications.

Clogg, R. (1992) *A Concise History of Greece*. Cambridge: Cambridge University Press.

Codaccioni, M. (1998) 'Le Groupe Revendiquant l'Assassinat du Prefet de Corse Menace "de Nouvelles Actions"'. *Le Monde* 23 September: 36.

Cohen, P. J. (1996) *Ending the War and Securing the Peace in Former Yugoslavia*. In S.G. Mestrovic (ed.), *Genocide After Emotion: Post-Emotional Balkan War*. London: Routledge.

Constas, D. and Stavrou, G. S. (eds) (1995) *Greece Prepares for the Twenty-first Century*. Baltimore: Johns Hopkins University Press.

Coulby, D. (1997a) 'Geopolitics, Language Education and Citizenship in the Baltic States: Estonia, Latvia and Lithuania'. In D. Coulby, C. Jones and J. Gundata (eds), *Intercultural Education: The World Yearbook of Education 1997*. London: Kogan Page.

Coulby, D. (1997b) 'Language and Citizenship in Latvia, Lithuania and Estonia: Education and the Brinks of Warfare'. *European Journal of Intercultural Studies 82*.

Coulby, D. and Bash, L. (1991) *Contradiction and Conflict: the 1988 Education Act in Action*. London: Cassell.

Coulby, D. and Jones, C. (1995) *Postmodernity and European Education Systems: Centralist Knowledge and Cultural Diversity*. Stoke on Trent: Trentham.

Coulby, D. and Jones, C. (1996) 'Postmodernity, Education and European Identities'. *Comparative Education and Postmodernity: Comparative Education Special Number 18, 32* (2): 171–84.

Coulby, D. and Ward, S. (eds) (1996) *The Primary Core National Curriculum: Education Policy into Practice* (2nd edn) London: Cassell.

Coulby, D., Cowen, R. and Jones, C. (eds) (2000) *The World Yearbook of Education 2000: Education in Times of Transition*. London: Kogan Page.

Coulby, J. and Coulby, D. (1995) 'Pupil Participation in the Social and Educational

Processes of a Primary School'. In P. Garner and S. Sandow (eds), *Advocacy, Self-Advocacy and Special Needs*. London: David Fulton.

Cowen, R. (ed.) (1996a) *The World Yearbook of Education 1996: The Evaluation of Systems of Higher Education*. London: Kogan Page.

Cowen, R. (1996b) 'Comparative Education and Post-Modernity'. *Comparative Education, 22, Special No. 180 (2)*.

Cowen, R. (1998) *The State, Civil Society and Economies: The University and the Politics of Space*. Paper presented at the CESE Conference on State, Market, Civil Society, Groningen.

Cucos, C. (1997) 'Interculturalism in Romania: the Metamorphosis of a Post-Totalitarian Society'. *European Journal of Intercultural Studies, 8* (3): 257–66.

Daniels, H. and Garner, P. (eds) (1999) *World Yearbook of Education 1999: Inclusive Education*. London: Kogan Page.

Delanty, G. (1995) *Inventing Europe: Idea, Identity, Reality*. London: Macmillan.

Department for Education and Employment (1998) *Teachers: Meeting the Challenge of Change*. (Cm 4164 ed.) London: Stationery Office.

Department for Education and Employment. (1999) *Press Release 208/99: Blunkett Unveils Proposals for National Curriculum from 2000* (press release) London: Department for Education and Employment.

Derrida, J. (1994) *Specters of Marx: The State of the Debt, the Work of Mourning, and the New International*. New York and London: Routledge.

Dewey, J. (1944) *Democracy and Education*. New York: Free Press.

Diaz-Andreu, M. and Champion, T. (eds) (1996) *Nationalism and Archaeology in Europe*. London: UCL.

Dixon, B. (1990) *Playing Women False*. Stoke on Trent: Trentham.

Done, K. (1998) 'Unification a Slow Process'. *Financial Times* 21 October: Survey II.

Dreifelds, J. (1996) *Latvia in Transition*. Cambridge: Cambridge University Press.

Dwyer, C. and Meyer, A. (1995) 'The Institutionalisation of Islam in the Netherlands and in the UK: the Case of Islamic Schools'. *new community*, 21 (1): 37–54.

Ellin, N. (1996) *Postmodern Urbanism*. Oxford: Blackwell.

European Bureau for Lesser Used Languages (1996) *North Frisia and Saterland: Frisian Between Marsh and Moor*. Brussels: EBLUL.

Fernandez-Armesto, F. (ed.) (1997) *The Times Guide to the Peoples of Europe (Revised Edition)* London: Times.

Feyerabend, P. (1978a) *Against Method*. London: Verso.

Feyerabend, P. (1978b) *Science in a Free Society*. London: Verso.

Fischer-Galati, S. (1991) *20th Century Romania*. New York: Columbia University Press.

Flouris, G. (1995) 'The Image of Europe in the Curriculum of the Greek Elementary School'. In G. Bell (ed.), *Educating European Citizens: Citizenship, Values and the European Dimension*. London: David Fulton.

Flouris, G. (1996) *Global Dimensions in the Educational Legislation, Social Studies Curriculum and Textbooks of the Greek Compulsory Education (Grades1–9)*: unpublished.

Flouris, G. (1997) 'Global Dimensions in the Educational Legislation, Social Studies Curriculum and Textbooks of Greek Compulsory Education (Grades 1–9)'. *Mediterranean Journal of Educational Studies, 2* (2): 17–39.

Flouris, G. (1998) 'Human Rights Curricula in the Formation of a European Identity: the Cases of Greece, England and France'. *European Journal of Intercultural Studies, 9* (1): 93–109.

Ford, J. et al. (1982) *Special Education and Social Control: Invisible Disasters*. London: Routledge and Kegan Paul.

Foucault, M. (1967) *Madness and Civilisation: a History of Insanity in the Age of Reason*. London: Tavistock.

Foucault, M. (1979) *Discipline and Punish: The Birth of the Prison*. Harmondsworth: Penguin.

Gamini, G. (1999) 'Guns in School Draw Ovation'. *Times Educational Supplement* 9 July: 25.

Garner, P. and Sandow, S. (eds) (1995) *Advocacy, Self-Advocacy and Special Needs*. London: David Fulton.

Georgiadou, V. (1995) 'Greek Orthodoxy and the Politics of Nationalism'. *International Journal of Politics, Culture and Society* 9 (2): 295–315.

Glass, N. (1999) 'Ministry in Dock over Racism Against Gypsies'. *Times Educational Supplement* 25 June: 24.

Grace, G. (1978) *Teachers, Ideology and Control: A Study in Urban Education*. London: Routledge and Kegan Paul.

Grant, N. (1994) 'Multicultural Societies in the European Community – the Odd Case of Scotland'. *European Journal of Intercultural Studies,* 5 (1): 51–9.

Grant, N. (1997) 'Intercultural Education in the UK'. In D. Coulby, J. Gundara and C. Jones (eds), *World Yearbook of Education*. London: Kogan Page.

Haarmann, H. (1995) 'Multilingualism and Ideology: the Historical Experiment of Soviet Language Politics'. *European Journal of Intercultural Studies* 5 (3): 6–17.

Hale, J. (1993) *The Civilisation of Europe in the Renaissance*. London: Harper Collins.

Hargreaves, D. H. *et al.* (1975) *Deviance in Classrooms*. London: Routledge and Kegan Paul.

Harvey, D. (1989) *The Condition of Postmodernity: an Enquiry into the Origins of Cultural Change*. Oxford: Blackwell.

Harvie, C. (1994) *The Rise of Regional Europe*. London: Routledge and Kegan Paul.

Hazecamp, J. L. and Popple, K. (eds) (1997) *Racism in Europe: A Challenge for Youth Policy and Youth Work*. London: UCL.

Hicks, D. and Slaughter, R. (eds) (1998) *The World Yearbook of Education 1998: Futures Education*. London: Kogan Page.

Hirst, P. and Peters, R. S. (1970) *The Logic of Education*. London: Routledge and Kegan Paul.

Hobsbawm, E. and Ranger, T. (eds) (1983) *The Invention of Tradition*. Cambridge: Cambridge University Press.

Hodge, R. and Kress, G. (1993) *Language as Ideology*. (2nd Edition) London: Routledge and Kegan Paul.

Hooper, J. (1995) *The New Spaniards*. Harmondsworth: Penguin.

Hungarian Ministry of Culture and Communication (1995) *Multicultural Education Development Scheme in Hungary*. Budapest.

Ignatieff, N. (1994) *Blood and Belonging: Journeys into the New Nationalism*. London: Vintage.

Illich, I. (1976) *Limits to Medicine: Medical Nemesis: The Expropriation of Health*. Harmondsworth: Penguin.

Israel, J. I. (1995) *The Dutch Republic, its Rise, Greatness and Fall 1477–1806*. Oxford: Clarendon.

Jameson, F. (1991) *Postmodernism or the Cultural Logic of Late Capitalism*. London: Verso.

Jaraunsch, K. H. *et al.* (1997) 'The Presence of the Past: Culture, Opinion, and Identity in Germany'. In K. H. Jarausch (ed.), *After Unity: Reconfiguring German Identities*. Providence: Berghahn.

119

Jarausch, K. H. (ed.) (1997) *After Unity: Reconfiguring German Identities*. Providence: Berghahn.

Jones, K. (1989) *Right Turn: The Conservative Revolution in Education*. London: Hutchinson Radius.

Joseph, G. G. (1992) *The Crest of the Peacock: Non-European Roots of Mathematics*. Harmondsworth: Penguin.

Judah, T. (1997) *The Serbs: History, Myth and the Destruction of Yugoslavia*. London: Yale University Press.

Kallio, V. (1994) *Finland: A Cultural Outline* (Herring, P. Trans.) Helsinki: Werner Soderstrom.

Kamin, L. J. (1974) *The Science and Politics of IQ*. New York: John Wiley.

Karaflogka, A. (1997) *Religion, Church and the State in Contemporary Greece: A People's Perspective*. Paper presented at the IV International Conference on Church–State Relations in Eastern and Central Europe, Krakow.

Keegan, J. (1993) *A History of Warfare*. London: Pimlico.

Kenaway, J. (1996) 'The Information Superhighway and Postmodernity: the Social Promise and the Social Price'. *Comparative Education and Postmodernity (Special Number 18), 22* (2): 217–32.

Khazanov, A. K. (1995) *After the USSR: Ethnicity, Nationalism and Politics in the Commonwealth of Independent States*. Madison: University of Wisconsin Press.

Kiernan, V. G. (1998) *Colonial Empires and Armies*. Stroud: Sutton.

King, E. J. (1979) *Other Schools and Ours: Comparative Studies for Today*. London: Holt Rienart Winston.

King, R. (1998) 'Post-oil Crisis, post-Communism: New Geographies of International Migration'. In D. Pinder (ed.), *The New Europe; Economy, Society and Environment*. Chichester: John Wiley.

Knapp, M. S. and Woolverton, S. (1995) 'Social Class and Schooling'. In J. A. Banks and C. A. M. Banks (eds), *Handbook of Research on Multicultural Education*. New York: Macmillan.

Kontogiannopoulou-Polydories, G. and Zambeta, E. (1997) 'Greece'. In M. Wilson (ed.), *Women in Educational Management: A European Perspective*: 78–96. London: Paul Chapman.

Labov, W. (1969) 'The Logic of Non-Standard English'. *Georgetown Monographs on Language and Linguistics, 22*: 1–31.

Lamawaima, K. T. (1995) 'Educating Native Americans'. In J. A. Banks and C. A. M. Banks (eds), *Handbook of Research on Multicultural Education*. New York: Macmillan.

Lash, S. and Urry, J. (1994) *Economies of Signs and Space*. London: Sage.

Lawton, D. (1988) *Education, Culture and the National Curriculum*. London: Hodder and Stoughton.

Lazardis, G. (1996) 'Immigration to Greece: A Critical Evaluation of Greek Policy'. *new community*, 22 (2): 335–48.

Lepkowska, D. (1998) 'Muslims Gain Equality of Funding'. *Times Educational Supplement* 16 January: 18.

Lieven, A. (1993) *The Baltic Revolution: Estonia, Latvia, Lithuania and the Path to Independence*. New Haven: Yale University Press.

Lieven, A. (1998) *Chechnya: Tombstone of Russian Power*. New Haven and London: Yale University Press.

Lodge, D. (1990) *After Bakhtin*. London: Routledge and Kegan Paul.

Lyotard, J. F. (1984) *The Postmodern Condition: A Report on Knowledge*. Manchester: Manchester University Press.

Macdonald, I. (1989) *Murder in the Playground: The Report of the Macdonald Inquiry into Racism and Racial Violence in Manchester Schools*. London: Longsight.

McDonald, C. (1999) 'Roma in the Romanian Educational System: Barriers and Leaps of Faith'. *European Journal of Intercultural Studies (The Education of Roma Children)* 10 (2): 183–200.

McLellan, D. (ed.) (1977) *Karl Marx: Selected Writings*. London: Oxford University Press.

Mackey, S. (1997) 'Nationalist Hitch to History Relaunch'. *Times Educational Supplement* 14 November: 21.

Marsden, D. and Marsden, P. R. (1995) 'Work, Labour Markets and Vocational Preparation: Anglo-German Comparisons of Training in Intermediate Skills'. In L. Bash and A. Green (eds), *The 1995 World Yearbook of Education*. London: Kogan Page.

Marshall, J. (1999) 'Chirac's 'Non' to Local Dialects'. *Times Educational Supplement* 9 July: 24.

Massialas, B. G. (1995) *The Quest for a European Identity: The Case of Education in Greece*. Paper presented at the Conference of the Comparative and International Education Society, Boston, Mass.

Massialas, B. G. and Flouris, G. (1994) *Education and the Emerging Concept of National Identity in Greece*. Paper presented at the Comparative and International Education Society, San Diego, Calif.

Mazower, M. (1998) *Dark Continent: Europe's Twentieth Century*. Harmondsworth: Allen Lane.

Ministry of Culture and Education (Hungary) (1995) *Multicultural Development Scheme in Hungary*. Budapest.

Murphy, D. (1992) *Transylvania and Beyond*. London: John Murray.

Neef, D. (ed.) (1998) *The Knowledge Economy*. Boston: Butterworth-Heinneman.

Nielsen, J. S. (1994) 'Muslims, Pluralism and the European Nation State'. *European Journal of Intercultural Studies* 5 (1): 18–22.

OFSTED (1999) *Special Education 1994–98: A Review of Special Schools, Secure Units and Pupil Referral Units in England*. London: The Stationery Office.

Overy, R. (1998) *Russia's War*. Harmondsworth: Allen Lane.

Parker-Jenkins, M. (1991) 'Muslim Matters: the Educational Needs of the Muslim Child'. *new community* 17 (4): 569–82.

Parker-Jenkins, M. (1994) *Social Justice: Educating Muslim Children*. Nottingham: School of Education Nottingham University.

Pavkovic, A. (1997) *The Fragmentation of Yugoslavia: Nationalism in a Multinational State*. Basingstoke: Macmillan.

Pettifer, J. (1994) *The Greeks: The Land and the People Since the War*. Harmondsworth: Penguin.

Pinder, D. (ed.) (1998) *The New Europe: Economy, Society and Environment*. Chichester: John Wiley.

Pollis, A. (1992) 'Greek National Identity: Religious Minorities, Rights and European Norms'. *Journal of Modern Greek Studies* 10 (2): 171–95.

Popkewitz, T. (1997) *A Changing Terrain of Knowledge and Power: a Social Epistemology of Educational Research*. Israel.

121

Popkewitz, T. S. (1999) 'Reconstituting Ethnography: Social Exclusion, Post-Modern Social Theory, and the Study of Teacher Education'. In C. A. Grant (ed.), *Multicultural Research: a Reflective Engagement with Race, Class, Gender and Sexual Orientation*. London: Falmer.

Psomiades, H. and Thomadaki, S. (1993) 'Greece, the New Europe and the Changing International Order'. New York: Pella Publications.

Rady, M. (1992) *Romania in Turmoil*. London: I. B. Tauris.

Rafferty, F. (1998) 'Small Classes, no Computers'. *Times Educational Supplement* July: 22.

Rattansi, A. and Westwood, S. (eds) (1994) *Racism, Modernity and Identity: On the Western Front*. Cambridge: Polity.

Rich, V. (1998a) 'Angry Minority Withdraws Support'. *Times Educational Supplement* 25 September: 13.

Rich, V. (1998b) 'Parties Clash over Ethnic University'. *Times Educational Supplement* 17 July: 9.

Richards, C. (1995) *The New Italians*. Harmondsworth: Penguin.

Romaniszyn, K. (1996) 'The Invisible Community: Undocumented Polish Workers in Athens'. *new community*, 23 (2): 321–33.

Rosandic, R. and Pesic, V. (eds) (1994) *Warfare, Patriotism, Patriarchy: the Analysis of Elementary School Textbooks*. Belgrade: Centre for Anti-War Action MOST.

Royal Ministry of Education, Research, and Church Affairs (Norway) (1997) *Core Curriculum for Primary, Secondary and Adult Education in Norway*. Oslo: National Centre for Educational Resources.

Rudge, L. (1998) '"I am nothing" – Does it Matter? A Critique of Current Religious Education Policy and Practice in England on Behalf of the Silent Majority'. *British Journal of Religious Education, 20* (3): 155–65.

Sandow, S. (1994) *Whose Special Need? Some Perceptions of Special Educational Needs*. London: Paul Chapman.

Sandow, S. (1995) 'Parents and Schools: Devleoping a Partnership Approach to Advocacy'. In P. Garner and S. Sandow (eds), *Advocacy, Self-Advocacy and Special Needs*. London: David Fulton.

Sarwar, G. (1984) *Muslims and Education in the UK*. London: The Muslim Education Trust.

Sarwar, G. (1993) *British Muslims and Schools*. London: The Muslim Education Trust.

Sharp, R. (1980) *Knowledge, Ideology and the Politics of Schools: Towards a Marxist Analysis of Education*. London: Routledge and Kegan Paul.

Silova, I. (1996) 'De-Sovietisation of Russian Textbooks Made Visible'. *European Journal of Intercultural Studies, 7* (2): 35–45.

Simon, B. (1971) *Intelligence, Psychology and Education: A Marxist Critique*. London: Lawrence and Wishart.

Smith, R. and Wexler, P. (eds) (1995) *After Postmodernism: Education, Politics and Identity*. London: Falmer.

Stamers, G. (1993) *Latvia Today*. Riga: Latvian Institute of International Affairs.

Supple, C. (1993) *From Prejudice to Genocide: Learning about the Holocaust*. London: Trentham.

Szabio, L. T. (1993) 'Values and Value Conflicts in Hungarian Education: The Case of the National Core Curriculum – An Unfinished Story'. *European Journal of Intercultural Studies, 4* (1): 57–64.

Szaday, C. (1994) 'Schooling in Multicultural Switzerland'. *European Journal of Intercultural Studies, 5* (1): 38–50.

Szasz, T. S. (1972) *The Myth of Mental Illness*. St Albans: Paladin.

Tomlinson, S. (1981) *Educational Subnormality – a Study in Decision Making*. London: Routledge and Kegan Paul.

Tomlinson, S. (1982) *A Sociology of Special Education*. London: Routledge and Kegan Paul.

Tsoucalas, C. (1993) 'Greek National Identity in an Integrated Europe and a Changing World Order'. In H. Psomiades and S. Thomadakis (eds), *Greece, The New Europe and the Changing International Order*. New York: Pella.

Tyler, R. W. (1949) *Basic Principles of Curriculum and Instruction*. London: University of Chicago Press.

UNDP (United Nations Development Programme) (1995) *Latvia Human Development Report*. Riga: UNDP.

Usher, R. and Edwards, R. (1994) *Postmodernism and Education*. London: Routledge.

Welsh Office (1995) *The Welsh Language: Children and Education*. Cardiff: Welsh Office.

Westwood, S. (1994) 'Racism, Mental Illness and the Politics of Identity'. In A. Rattansi and S. Westwood (eds), *Racisms, Modernity and Identity: On the Western Front*. London: Polity.

Wexler, P. (1995) 'After Postmodernism; A New Age Social Theory in Education'. In R. Smith and P. Wexler (eds), *After Postmodernism: Education, Politics and Identity*. London: Falmer.

Wichmann, J. (1998) 'The Transformation of Educational Systems in Central and Eastern Europe: Some Prospects and Problems'. In A. M. Kazamias and M. G. Spillane (eds), *Education and the Structuring of European Space*: 269–83. Athens: Seirios Editions.

Young, M. F. D. (ed.) (1971) *Knowledge and Control: New Directions for the Sociology of Education*. London: Collier Macmillan.

Young, R. J. C. (1995a) *Colonial Desire: Hybridity in Theory, Culture and Race*. London: Routledge.

Young, R. (1995b) 'Liberalism, Postmodernism, Critical Theory and Politics'. In R. Smith and P. Wexler (eds) *After Postmodernism: Education, Politics and Identity*. London: Falmer.

Zambeta, E. (1999) *Crisis and Reform in Greek Education – a Text Analysis of Law 2525/1997* (Unpublished). Athens: University of Athens.

Zukin, S. (1988) *Loft Living: Culture and Capital in Urban Change*. London: Radius.

Zukin, S. (1991) *Landscapes of Power: from Detroit to Disney World*. Berkeley: University of California Press.

Zukin, S. (1995) *The Cultures of Cities*. Oxford: Blackwell.

# Index

India 63, 98
industrial action 19, 23, 37
industrial revolution 62, 70, 93, 100
*Information Age: Economy, Society and Culture* 73
information and communications technology
    (ICT) 3. 4, 47, 60, 62, 63, 64, 65, 66, 68,
    72; cost of in education 70
Inguchetia 38; Inguchetians 8
Inner London Education Authority (ILEA)
    23, 24, 107
Inquisition, Holy 36
inspection of schools 16, 17, 19, 58, 71, 72
intelligence 80, 81; political construct 82; *see
    also* science of intelligence
internationalism, Soviet 8, 9
inward investment 6, 69
Ireland 31–32, 43, 44, 45, 58, 69, 94, 95
Iron Curtain, collapse of 3, 31
isolationism 9
Israel 31
Italy 38, 43, 57, 92, 93; Fascist 21; national
    diversity of 28–9

Jameson, F. 55, 103, 115
Japan 6, 35, 61, 97
Jaraunsch, K. H. 20, 28
Jones, C. 3, 11, 23, 52, 56, 103, 104, 110, 115
Judah, G. G. 9, 91, 94
just-in-time learning 68

Kamin, L. J. 82, 87
Karaflogka, A. 30, 95
Khazanov, A. K. 8, 11, 38, 43
Kiernan, V. G. 88, 102
King, E. J. 10, 37
*King John* 91
knowledge 1, 105; conflicts over 40;
    construction/production of 2, 19, 62, 64;
    different from state to state 2; diversity
    39–41, 80; ethnocentric 52; and identity
    *x*; lies, trivia, ignorance and prejudice 2;
    myth of *ix*; paradigms of 40; political/state
    control of *ix*, *x*, 10, 12–24, 26–41,
    109–14; politicized 20, 21, 22, 53; and
    religion *x*; and special educational needs *x*;
    state knowledge 103–14; status of
    branches 47; as trading commodity 6,
    62–4, 97; and warfare *x*, 88–102
*Knowledge and Control: New Directions for the
    Sociology of Education* 24, 106

knowledge economy *x*, 2, 4, 6, 40, 60–73;
    and curricula 6, 9; value of in UK 64
*Knowledge Economy, The* 73
knowledge protocols 13, 66, 69, 80–6, 105,
    110, 111, 112; stigmatizing atypical
    groups 76–7, 82
knowledge selection 12–15, 111
knowledge society; relation to economy and
    power 9–10
knowledge systems 1, 55, 74–9, 86; deviant 2
knowledge, centralized: threat to minority
    cultures 1; *see also* curricula
knowledge, right to 14
knowledge, state: victims of 1, 2
Kontogiannopoulou-Polydores, G. 19, 46
Kosovo 5, 6, 101; *see also* Grand Alliance
Kosovo, Battle of 9, 91
Kress, G. 112

labelling 83–4
Labour party (UK) 23, 24; *see also* New
    Labour
language 111–14: aspirations to linguistic
    distinctiveness 27; conflicts over 36, 38,
    40; linguistic imperialism 23, 28;
    linguistic loyalties 31, 32, 36; linguistic
    rights 21; nationalism 8, 9, 27–8, 29, 56,
    110; *see also* asymmetric bilingualism
languages 20, 34, 35, 47, 48, 49, 69,
    89–92; Arabic 39; Bangladeshi 39;
    Basque 27, 112; Castilian Spanish 28,
    37; Catalan 21, 27, 28, 37 112
    (campaigns to eliminate 37); Chinese 91,
    39; Cornish 27, 36; Danish 28; Dutch
    35; English 5, 8, 9, 13, 18, 21, 48, 56,
    63, 65, 69, 90, 91, 111, 112, 113;
    Finnish 28; French 112; Gallician 112;
    Gaelic 27; German 5, 32, 36; Gujerati
    39; Hindi 39; Hungarian 32, 36; Latvian
    21; Manx 27; Occitan 27; Roma 32, 36;
    Romanian 32, 36; Russian 8, 21, 90, 91,
    112; Scots 27; Swahili 39; Turkish 39,
    89, 90; Urdu 39; Welsh 27, 36, 37
    (campaign to eliminate 36) (state support
    for 36) (compulsory teaching of 36);
    Yiddish 31
languages, number spoken by pupils in
    London schools 38
Lash, S. 62, 63
Latvia 4, 8, 10, 21, 33, 38, 39, 49, 56–7, 90,

Thessalonika 30, 31
Three Rs 54
topic-based approaches 57
tourism 5, 29, 49
tradition 20, 34, 45, 50–2, 94; creation of 9,
    42–59
traditional values in curricula 9, 64
transition: costs of 4–5; differences in
    different regions 4; time scale of 5
transitions: in Eastern Europe 4–6, 21; in
    Europe *ix*, 3–11; in Western Europe 6–10
trans-national corporations 3, 61
transparency 18
Transylvania 20, 28, 32, 36
Turkey 30, 89, 101; Turkish empire 40

Ullah, Ahmed Iqbal, murder of 14
UNDP 9, 33
unemployment 66, 68
United Kingdom (UK) 3, 21, 22, 23, 27,
    31, 36, 37, 38, 46, 47, 63, 67, 69, 82,
    94, 106, 110, 112; national diversity 27,
    92; religious differences 27; Secretary of
    State for Education and Science 21; reli-
    giously-affiliated schools 31, 34, 35, 42,
    43, 44, 45, 65, 66, 70, 71, 72, 76, 94
United States of America 1, 2, 3, 6, 10, 19,
    30, 60, 61, 63, 64, 66, 67, 69, 70, 71,
    78, 94, 97, 99, 106, 112; genocide 94;
    uncontested power of 4, 6
universities 64, 78; control less rigid than
    schools 107; and gender 46; international
    competition for students 63–4; and
    knowledge economy 64–6, 107; and
    Marxism 104; and militarism 88, 92, 96,
    97, 99, 101; and nationalism/racism 9,
    12, 34; controlled by religious institu-
    tions 43, 44, 95; *see also* higher education
urbanization 37, 38
Urry, J. 62, 63
Usher, R. 56, 103

value systems 1, 45, 55
values, political 22
victims of curricula/state knowledge 1, 2, 55
Vilnius 31; University of 45
violence *see* state's monopoly of, genocide,
    ethnic cleansing
Vlaams Bloc (Belgium) 29
vocational skills *see* skills for workplace

Vojvodina 4, 32
Volga Germans 8, 38
Vukovar 89

Wales 23, 27, 36, 37, 94, 110; assembly 27,
    36
Wallachia 32, 38
war: and Europe 2, 88; and knowledge
    88–102; military training 99–100; in
    national literature 91; *see also* civil wars
*Warfare, Patriotism, Patriarchy: The Analysis of
    Elementary School Textbooks* 102
Weber, M. 66
Western attitudes: triumphalism 7; neglect
    of non-Western knowledge 13, 51, 52,
    54–5, 58
Wexler, P. 56, 103
Whitehall *see* civil servants
Wichmann, J. 110
women 7, 39, 74, 93, 100
workplace 46, 47; *see also* skills
*World Yearbook of Education 1996: the Evalu-
    ation of Systems of Higher Education* 115
*World Yearbook of Education 1999: Inclusive
    Education* 87
*World Yearbook of Education 2000: Education in
    Times of Transition* 11
worldwide web 66, 70

xenophobia 9, 12, 29, 92, 93, 94, 96, 98, 101

Yalta agreement 31
young children, pressures on 48
Young, M. F. D. 24, 34, 103, 106
youth culture 47
Yugoslavia, former 5, 7, 27, 31, 32, 35, 92,
    93, 94

Zambeta, E. 19, 46, 72, 93
Zukin, S. 63